CW01651172

ACCA

Advanced Performance Management (APM)

Pocket Notes

KAPLAN PUBLISHING

British library cataloguing-in-publication data

A catalogue record for this book is available from the British Library.

Published by:
Kaplan Publishing UK
Unit 2 The Business Centre
Molly Millars Lane
Wokingham
Berkshire
RG41 2QZ

ISBN 978-1-83735-041-4

Printed and bound in Great Britain.

Acknowledgments:

This product contains material that is ©Financial Reporting Council Ltd (FRC). Adapted and reproduced with the kind permission of the Financial Reporting Council. For further information, please visit www.frc.org.uk or call +44 (0)20 7492 2300.

Contents

Introduction to the syllabus

The aim of this paper is to apply relevant knowledge and skills and to exercise professional judgement in selecting and applying strategic management accounting techniques in different business contexts, to contribute to the planning, control and evaluation of the performance of an organisation and its strategic and operational development.

Strong underpinning knowledge is required from Performance Measurement (PM). APM is a step up from PM and focuses on interpretation and application of the topics.

APM builds on knowledge gained in Performance Management (PM). It develops key aspects introduced at the PM level with a greater focus on linking the syllabus topics together and evaluation of the key topics and techniques.

Assumed knowledge from PM
• Risk • Environmental management accounting (EMA) • Alternative budgeting methods • Absorption costing and activity-based costing (ABC) • Beyond budgeting • Standard costing and variances • Forecasting • Information and data

- Big data
- Data analytics
- Management information systems (MIS)
- Financial performance measures
- Divisional performance measures
- Transfer pricing
- Not-for-profit organisations
- Non-financial performance indicators
- Balanced scorecard
- Building Block model

APM also includes knowledge contained in the Strategic Business Leader (SBL) exam but it is not a problem if you are yet to study for this exam and there is no expectation that you will have any SBL knowledge in place. It is important to draw a distinction between the two exams. You need to approach the common topics from an APM perspective, i.e. how do they influence performance management and measurement.

Main capabilities

On successful completion of this exam, candidates should be able to:

A Use **stategic planning and control models** to plan and monitor organisational performance

B Identify and evaluate the design features of effective **performance management information** and monitoring **systems and** recognise the impact of **developments in technology** on performance measurement and management systems

C Apply appropriate **strategic performance measurement** techniques in evaluating and improving organisational performance

D Advise clients and senior management on strategic business **performance evaluation**

E Apply a range of **professional skills** in adressing requirements within the Advanced Performance Management exam, and in preparation for, or to support, current work experience

F **Employability and technology skills**

The examination

Format of the exam	Number of marks
Section A – one compulsory question	50
Section B – two compulsory questions worth 25 marks each	50
Total	100

- The exam is a 3 hour 15 minutes computer based examination (CBE).
- The pass mark is 50%.
- Technical syllabus sections A, B and C (not D) are examinable in Section A.
- In Section B, one question will include technical marks mainly from syllabus section D. The other question will include technical marks from any other technical syllabus section(s).
- There will be 10 professional marks available in Section A and 5 professional marks available in each Section B question.

Professional skills

The inclusion of this syllabus area reflects ACCA's continued focus on ensuring that the professional accountants of the future have the right blend of **technical and professional skills**, coupled with an **ethical mindset**.

The APM exam will expect candidates to demonstrate the following Professional Skills:

Professional Skill	Section A (10 marks)	Section B (5 marks/question)
Communication	All four Professional Skills will be examined.	Not examined
Analysis and Evaluation		Each question will contain a minimum of two professional skills from Analysis and Evaluation, Scepticism and Commercial Acumen.
Scepticism		
Commercial Acumen		

- Each of the four professional skills has a number of **leadership capabilities** associated and these will be used to **allocate marks** in each exam question as appropriate.
- **Professional skills marks are earned as you work through the technical marks** by providing a comprehensive and relevant response to the technical requirements. Therefore, **time should be allocated based on the technical marks** available.

Employability and technology skills

By studying for ACCA exams, candidates will be equipped with not only technical syllabus knowledge and professional skills, but also practical, applied software skills. The employability and technology skills syllabus area is included within the syllabus to acknowledge this acquired skillset.

The CBE software will **replicate the work that is performed by accountants in a typical workplace**. It will be used across the syllabus to support a candidate's answer by providing suitable response options for different types of answers. These response options will be most suitable in the following instances:

- For **discursive answers**: it is best to use the **word processing** option
- For **calculations**: it is best to use the **spreadsheet** option.

ACCA candidates can access the **ACCA's Exam Practice Platform** to practice attempting questions using the CBE software. It is imperative that candidates are familiar with the software before attempting the exam.

Key study tips

Ensure you review prior knowledge from PM and understand that topics common to both APM and SBL will focus on the use of models for performance management and measurement.

Revise the course as you work through it and leave sufficient time before the exam for final revision.

Cover the whole syllabus and pay attention to areas where your knowledge is weak.

Practice exam standard questions under timed conditions. Attempt all the different styles of questions you may be asked and practice answering questions using the CBE Practice Platform.

Read the APM articles on the ACCA website and read good newspapers and professional journals.

Key reasons for failure in APM

Poor exam technique	Technical weaknesses
• Repeating learned facts only. • No relation to scenario. • Not answering the question. • Not applying knowledge to the scenario. • Lack of practice.	• Inability to do fundamental calculations. • Poor use of models. • No focus on performance management and measurement. • Poor interpretation of data. • Not understanding differences between key principles.

Quality and accuracy are of the utmost importance to us so if you spot an error in any of our products, please send an email to mykaplanreporting@kaplan.com with full details, or follow the link to the feedback form in MyKaplan.

Our Quality Co-ordinator will work with our technical team to verify the error and take action to ensure it is corrected in future editions.

chapter

1

Introduction to performance management

In this chapter

- Planning and control.
- Strategic objectives, critical success factors and key performance indicators.
- The role of performance measures.
- Benchmarking.

Exam focus

This chapter sets the scene to Part A of the syllabus, **'strategic planning and control'**.

It looks at the strategic role of the management accountant as a discipline for planning and controlling performance so that the strategic objectives can be set, monitored and controlled. We will consider the difference between these two roles and look at the **different levels of planning and control** within an organisation as well as the **importance of performance measures** in checking towards the achievement of the plans set. A central part of this process is to understand how the **objectives** of the organisation link to the **critical success factors** (CSFs) and **key performance indicators** (KPIs).

Next, we will move onto benchmarking. An important aspect of strategic planning is to understand how to **benchmark** performance so that areas for performance improvement can be identified.

Planning and control

Planning and control are **fundamental aspects of performance management.**

Planning	Control
The organisation sets its objectives and decides how best to achieve them.	The organisation monitors achievement of objectives and suggests any necessary corrective action.

The performance hierarchy is concerned with planning and control at different levels of the organisation:

A **mission statement** outlines the broad direction of an organisation, its reasons for existing and its values.'

Differences between strategic and operational planning and control

Strategic planning and control	Operational planning and control
Undertaken by senior managers.	Undertaken by operational managers.
Long-term, considering the whole organisation (and its divisions/departments) and all stakeholders.	Ensures objectives set at tactical level are achieved.
Information has an external focus and is commonly qualitative.	Information is detailed, task specific, mainly internal and largely quantitative.
Focus on planning not control.	Focus on control not planning to achieve short-term objectives.

Strategic planning is a **long-term**, top-down process and decisions may conflict with **short-term** localised **operational** decisions.

Strategic objectives, critical success factors and key performance indicators

The mission will be translated into a set of SMART, strategic objectives. Achievement of these objectives should ultimately help the organisation to achieve its mission.

Definition

Critical success factors (CSFs) are the vital areas 'where things must go right' for the organisation in order for them to achieve their strategic objectives.

CSFs can be **classified** as **monitoring or building** and also as **internal or external**.

There are different **sources** of CSFs. **For example industry or environmental factors** may drive the CSFs for an organisation.

Definition

Key performance indicators (KPIs) are the measures which indicate whether or not the CSFs are being achieved. Targets will be set for each KPI.

The role of performance measures

An organisation needs to establish SMART objectives and then key factors and processes will be identified that will enable it to achieve its objectives.

It is not enough merely to make plans and implement them.
The results of the plans have to be **measured**.

'What gets measured, gets done'
– i.e. the things that are measured get done much more often than the things that are not measured.

- Once measured, the results should be **compared** to the stated objectives.
- **Action** can then be taken to remedy any shortfalls in performance.

Benchmarking

Definition

Benchmarking aims to understand and evaluate the current position of the organisation in relation to **best practice** (products, services or processes) and to identify areas and means of performance improvement.

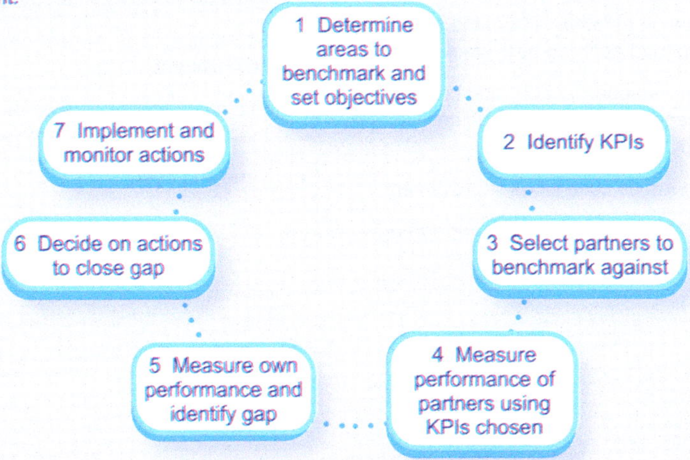

Benchmarking evaluation

Advantages	Disadvantages
• Helps to assess current strategic position. • Identifies gaps in performance and sets challenging but achievable targets. • A method of learning from the success of others and applying best practice. • Minimises complacency and provides an early warning sign of competitive disadvantage. • Encourages continuous improvement. • Can help in assessing generic strategy.	• Identifying best practice difficult. • Not forward looking. • Differences between areas benchmarked. • Potential for lack of staff/ management commitment. • Too much focus on areas benchmarked to the detriment of overall performance. • Time and cost.

Types of benchmarking

Type	Advantages	Disadvantages
Internal benchmarking is where another function or division of the organisation is used as the benchmark.	• Share best practice • Obtain detailed operational data • Integrates different parts of organisation	• May not be innovative • No external focus • Often involves non-financial data and this may be less robust
Competitor benchmarking uses a direct competitor in the same industry with the same or similar processes as the benchmark.	• Identify where other organisations have competitive advantage • Identify areas for improvement with a similar business	• Competitor may be reluctant to share information or may want something in return • May not identify how to gain competitive advantage
Process/activity benchmarking focuses on a similar process/activity in another organisation, which is not a direct competitor.	• Easier to obtain information from non-competitor • Solutions can still be innovative • Easier to translate lessons if done for generic activities	• May be difficult to translate lessons learned • Connecting organisations in different industries more difficult and different information systems may limit sharing

Exam focus

Exam sitting	Area examined	Question number
Mar/Jun 2023	What gets measured gets done	1(ii)
Dec 2022	Benchmarking	2(a)
Mar/Jun 2022	BCG and recommendation of KPIs	1(ii)
Sept/Dec 2021	Performance hierarchy, CSFs and KPIs	1(iv)
March/Jun 2021	Performance hierarchy, CSFs and KPIs	1(a)
Sept/Dec 2020	Performance hierarchy, CSFs and KPIs	1(i)
March 2020	Performance hierarchy, CSFs and KPIs	1(ii)
Sept/Dec 2019	Performance hierarchy, CSFs and KPIs	1(iii)
March/Jun 2019	Performance hierarchy, CSFs and KPIs	1(a)

chapter

2

Strategy and performance

In this chapter

- Strategic planning.
- Models used in the performance management process.

Exam focus

The next part of the chapter will look at some models (**SWOT, PEST, Porter's 5 Forces, Boston Consulting Group** (BCG) and **Porter's generic strategies**) used to assist in the performance management process.

Strategic planning

Strategic analysis

- External analysis to identify opportunities and threats.
- Internal analysis to identify strengths and weaknesses.
- Stakeholder analysis to identify key objectives and to assess power and interest of different groups.
- Gap analysis to identify the difference between desired and expected performance.

Strategic choice

- Strategies are required to 'close the gap'.
- Competitive strategy – for each business unit.
- Directions for growth – which markets/products should be invested in.
- Whether expansion should be achieved by organic growth, acquisition or some form of joint arrangement.

Strategic implementation

- Formulation of detailed plans and budgets.
- Target setting for KPIs.
- Monitoring and control.

Models used in the performance management process

SWOT analysis

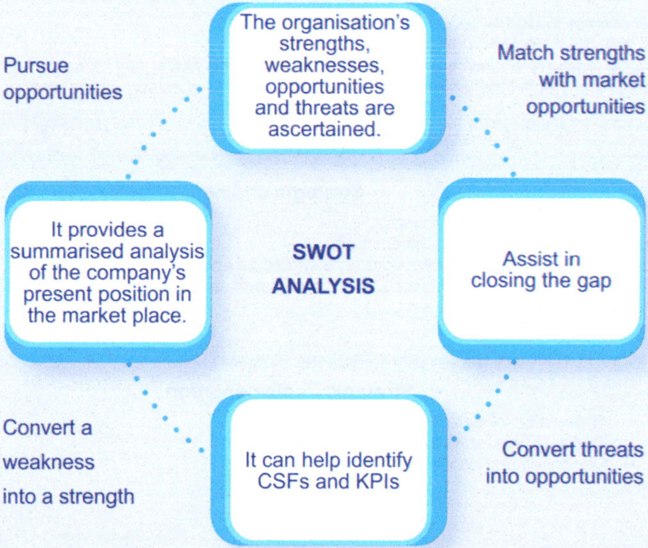

Tools for external analysis

(a) Porter's 5 forces

Industry level analysis looking at the pressures that determine how attractive the sector is.

It is important to **measure, manage** and **monitor** the forces using suitable performance indicators.

(b) PEST analysis

Approach to analysing the **macro-environment**:

- **Political influences and events**
- **Economic influences**
- **Social influences**
- **Technological influences**

As well as being used for strategic analysis, PEST can be used to **identify key performance management issues** such as:

- identification and exploitation of opportunities in the external environment
- identification and monitoring of threats, risk and uncertainty so that necessary action can be taken
- identification and monitoring of CSFs and KPIs relating to opportunities and risks.

Boston Consulting Group (BCG) matrix

- The matrix shows whether the firm has a balanced portfolio.
- Consider **how to manage different categories to optimise performance, what performance indicators are needed for each category** (and the **alignment of these indicators with the overall mission and objectives**).

Market growth	Relative market share: High	Relative market share: Low
High	**Star** • Is the high reinvestment being spent effectively? • Is market share being gained, held or eroded? • Is customer perception improving? • Are customer CSFs changing as the market grows? • Could measure profit or return on investment. • Is the star becoming a cash cow?	**Problem child** **Investment strategy** • Is market share being gained? • Effectiveness of promotional spend. **Divestment strategy** • Monitor contribution to see whether to exit quickly or divest slowly.
Low	**Cash cow** • Cash generator. Strategy is minimal investment to keep product going. • Is market share being eroded – could the cash cow be moving towards becoming a dog? • Measure net cash flow.	**Dog** • Monitor contribution to see whether to exit quickly or divest slowly. • Monitor market growth as an increase in the growth rate could justify retaining the product.

Advantages	Disadvantages
• Ensures a balanced portfolio. • Used to manage divisions in different ways. • Metrics set in line with analysis. • Looks at portfolio as a whole, rather than assessing the performance of each part separately. • Can be used to assess performance.	• Simplistic; only looks at market growth and relative market share. • Designed for portfolio analysis, not performance management. • Determining what 'high' and 'low' mean is difficult. • Does not consider links between parts of the organisation. • May encourage holding rather than growth strategy for cash cows.

Ansoff's matrix and its use in closing the performance planning gap

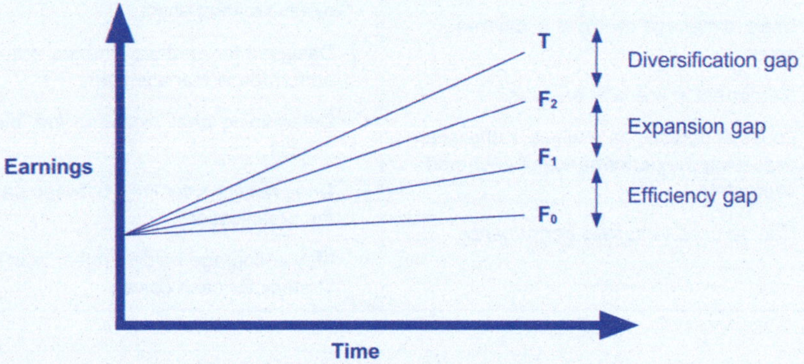

Key:

T = target

F_0 = initial forecast

F_1 = forecast after addressing efficiency gap

F_2 – forecast after addressing expansion gap

$T–F_0$ = **planning gap**

Ansoff represented the choices for closing the planning gap in the **product/market matrix:**

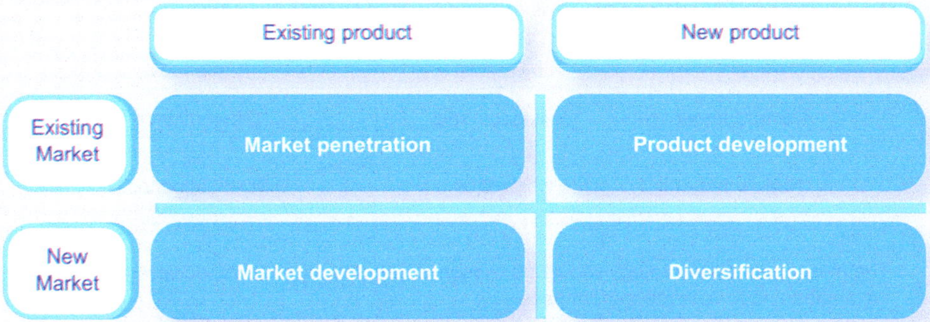

- **Market penetration** – Techniques include improved quality and efficiency (hence addresses **efficiency gap**), increased market activity and brand repositioning.
- **Product development** – Product modifications or innovations used to close **expansion gap** through fulfilment of customer needs not met by existing products.
- **Market development** – Used to close **expansion gap** by attempting to sell existing products to new customer segments or geographical regions.
- **Diversification** – Related (familiar market/industry) or unrelated (new market/industry) to close **diversification gap.**

Porter's generic strategies

An important part of strategic choice is deciding on what basis to compete.

	Lower cost	Higher cost
Broad target	Cost leadership	Differentiation
Narrow target	Focus: Cost focus	Focus: Differentiation focus

The most appropriate strategy should be chosen to help the organisation achieve competitive advantage and to optimise performance.

Exam focus

Exam sitting	Area examined	Question number
March/Jun 2021	5 forces and PEST	1(b)

chapter

3

Managing risk and uncertainty

In this chapter

- Risk and uncertainty.

Exam focus

In the final part of the chapter, we discuss the **risk and uncertainty** that exists in the environment and how these risks/ uncertainties can be measured and managed, including the impact of **different risk appetites of stakeholders**.

Risk and uncertainty

All organisations face risk and uncertainty.

Definitions

- **Risk** is the variability of possible returns. There are a number of possible outcomes and the probability of each outcome is **known**.
- **Uncertainty** is also the variability of possible returns. There are a number of possible outcomes and the probability of each outcome is **not known**.
- **Exogenous variables** originate from outside the organisation and are not controllable by it.
- **Endogenous variables** are factors under the control of management.

Four key tools are available for making decisions where there is an element of risk/uncertainty involved.

Risk technique	Suitability	Limitations
Expected values (EVs) – The average return if the decision is repeated again and again.	Organisation has a risk neutral approach to risk.	Not useful for one off decisions, if probabilities and/ or values of outcomes are uncertain/unknown, for non-risk neutral decision makers.
Maximax – Looks at the maximum return for each course of action and chooses the course of action with the highest maximum return.	Organisation is risk seeking and optimistic and can be used for one-off or repeated decisions.	May be considered overly optimistic since risks making a lower profit if the maximum outcome is not delivered.
Maximin – Looks at the minimum return for each course of action and chooses the course of action with the highest minimum return.	Organisation is risk averse and pessimistic and can be used for one-off or repeated decisions.	May be considered overly pessimistic since miss out on the possibility of making a bigger profit.
Mininmax regret – Looks at the maximum regret (opportunity cost) for each course of action and chooses the course of action that minimises the maximum regret.	Organisation does not want to make the wrong decision and miss out. Can be used for one-off or repeated decisions.	Risks making a lower profit.

It is important to consider the **risk appetite of stakeholders** when deciding on the most appropriate tool for decision making under risk/uncertainty.

Shareholders

- Commonly risk seeking. Prepared to take a risk, hold a portfolio of investments to spread risk – **maximax** suitable.
- However, shareholders in a company in financial distress may be more **risk averse or neutral – maximin or EVs** suitable.

Employees and managers

Should act in the best interests of shareholders but:

- may be **risk averse** if an unsuccessful outcome would impact their remuneration or job security – **maximin** preferred.
- may be **risk seeking** if a bonus or reward is offered for a high outcome – **maximax** preferred.

Venture capitalists

- Rational investors seeking **maximum return for minimum risk.**
- Hold a portfolio of investments, monitor progress against targets/to ensure exit strategy can be achieved and place employees on the management team to influence decisions – **maximax** suitable.

Banks

- **Conservative approach** to risk aiming to secure funds/returns – **maximin (or perhaps EVs)** suitable.

Exam focus

Exam sitting	Area examined	Question number
Sept/Dec 2019	Risk and uncertainty	3(b)(c)

chapter

4

Environmental, social and governance factors

In this chapter

- The impact of stakeholders.
- Environmental, social and governance (ESG) factors.
- Integrated reporting.
- Environmental management accounting (EMA).

Exam focus

Much of the focus of APM will be on profit seeking organisations and more specifically companies. Companies have the primary objective to maximise shareholder wealth. When considering how best to achieve this objective it can be easy to focus:

- primarily on the shareholders and not the other stakeholders and
- on managing and measuring financial performance (e.g. return on capital employed (ROCE) or gross profit margins) and/or more traditional non-financial areas of performance (e.g. employee and customer satisfaction, or product quality).

Although this focus is important, it is also necessary for organisations to understand how vital it is to consider a range of other issues when managing and measuring performance (such as environmental and social factors) and for an organisation to consider its different stakeholders and not just its shareholders.

The impact of stakeholders

Definition

A **stakeholder** is a group or individual who has an interest in what the organisation does, or an expectation of the organisation. As such, they may attempt to influence its mission, objectives and strategy.

- The primary objective of profit seeking organisations is to maximise shareholder wealth. However, an organisation (whether profit seeking or not-for-profit) must consider the needs of all of its stakeholders.
- There is an increasing recognition amongst stakeholders of the importance of sustainability and the impact of businesses on society and the environment. Stakeholders are interested in how an organisation is performing in these areas.

Definition

Corporate social responsibility (CSR) refers to the idea that a company should be sensitive to the needs of all stakeholders in its business operations and not just shareholders.

Stakeholder mapping (Mendelow's matrix)

Helps analyse the organisation's stakeholders and suggests possible strategies for each one. Used to manage stakeholders' conflicting demands and to establish priorities.

Steps to optimise performance

1. Identify all stakeholders and their needs/objectives.

↓

2. Consider the relative levels of power and interest of the stakeholders and plot these on the matrix.

↓

3. Evaluate, using the matrix, how the different stakeholders should be managed.

↓

4. Establish priorities (for example, prioritise 'key players').

↓

5. Manage conflicting demands

↓

6. Develop the mission and strategic objectives with the stakeholders' needs in mind.

↓

7. Establish CSFs and KPIs that are aligned to the achievement of the mission and strategic objectives.

↓

8. Translate the strategic objectives into tactical and operational objectives and establish performance measures for these.

Environmental, social and governance (ESG) factors

Definitions

ESG refers to the three central factors in measuring the sustainability and societal impact of an organisation and that help to determine the long-term performance of an organisation.

Ethics is a set of moral principles that examines the concept of right and wrong. It relates to behaviour expected by society, but not codified in law.

Business ethics is the application of ethical values to business behaviour. They are a key component of an organisation's ESG strategy.

Corporate governance (the '**G**' in 'ES**G**') is the set of processes and policies by which a company is directed, administered and controlled. It is concerned with the overall control and direction of a business so that the business's objectives are achieved in an acceptable manner by all stakeholders.

Sustainability is an important aspect of ESG and is a key focus of this chapter. Two possible definitions are:

- Development that meets the needs of the present without compromising the ability of future generations to meet their own needs.
- A need for organisations to focus on economic prosperity, environmental quality and social justice. Sometimes summarised as the **3 P's** of Planet (environmental), People (social) and Profit (economic).

Triple bottom line (TBL) accounting means expanding the traditional company reporting framework to take into account environmental and social performance in addition to economic performance.

ESG and performance management

Arguments for ESG	Arguments against ESG
• Help attract/retain customers. • Help attract a wider and/or higher calibre human resource base. • May reduce costs, fines, lawsuits and allow access to subsidies and government support. • Fulfil the needs of stakeholders who may otherwise join forces and increase power. • Can help attract investors and reduce risk resulting in cheaper finance. The above should improve long-term performance. • In addition to performance improvement, consideration of ESG factors is ethically correct.	• May conflict with a manager's duty to maximise shareholder wealth. • It could be argued that focusing on maximising shareholder wealth can be aligned with consideration of ESG issues. • Potential increased costs. • Lack of knowledge of the benefits, the actions to be taken and how these should be reported and measured. • Lack of skills and resources. • May have to turn away business from customers considered to be unethical. • It could be argued that it is enough to comply with relevant laws and regulations.

Introduction

Management accountants, as trusted advisors, will be at the heart of sustainability action. They will have a significant role in embedding performance measures in the area of sustainability into the core performance measurement process:

Identifying CSFs and establishing relevant KPIs → Measuring performance → Reporting and controlling performance

The modern management accountant will need to successfully combine traditional technical accounting skills with business, people, leadership and digital skills (all underpinned by ethics and professionalism) but is well positioned to meet the changing mandate and should view this as an opportunity.

Identifying CSFs and establishing relevant KPIs

The management accountant will work alongside the CEO to embed sustainability issues in the entire performance management process:

Mission
Sustainabilty should be a core part of the mission

→ **Strategic objectives**
SMART sustainabilty objectives aligned with the mission

→ **CSFs**
identify specific practices to achieve the strategic objectives

→ **KPIs and targets**
Assess how well an organisation is achieving its sustainability objectives

Features of a good KPI for sustainability:

- Actually measure sustainability
- Align with mission, objectives and CSFs
- Recognise interconnectedness between measures
- Balanced picture (good and bad)
- Focus on areas that have greatest potential impact
- Measure over time to identify trends
- Clear and consistent to aid benchmarking

Measuring performance

- Once appropriate KPIs have been established, the management accountant will have a role in collecting KPI data and transforming it into useful information so that sustainability can be measured.
- The management accountant will analyse the information to draw out patterns and insights for those who use the information.
- Information technology (IT) will assist with this.

Reporting and controlling performance

The UN climate change conference, COP26, was held in Autumn 2021. The creation of an **International Sustainability Standards Board (ISSB)** was announced at the conference, a major step towards globally aligned ESG reporting. ISSB standards will **provide the foundation for consistent and global ESG reporting standards** that will enable companies to report on ESG factors affecting their business. The standards are still in development but once in place they should act as a transformational event for ESG reporting.

However, at present, there is **no globally accepted framework for reporting** but **two possible frameworks** for sustainability reporting are **The Global Reporting Initiative (GRI) Standards** (best practice for reporting on a range of economic, environmental and social impacts) and **The United Nations' (UN) Sustainable Development Goals (SDGs)**(more detail below).

The United Nations' (UN) Sustainable Development Goals (SDGs)

The UN SDGs encourage countries to embed sustainability measures into their 'core' performance reporting. In 2015, the UN launched 17 SDGs to end poverty, fight inequality and justice and tackle climate change by 2030. Each **goal** has a related set of **targets** (169 in total) and **indicators**.

17 SDGs and 169 related targets is a lot. Organisations need to:

- Prioritise the choice of SDGs and related targets to those where they can make a meaningful contribution and should be ambitious.
- Focus on and pick out the SDGs and targets that are aligned to the mission and objectives (in which sustainability issues should be embedded).

Organisations need to **take steps to measure and monitor performance in order to keep on track of their commitments**. The **management accountant will have an important role** in this.

Integrated reporting

Definition

With Integrated Reporting (IR), instead of having environmental and social issues reported in a separate section of the annual report, or a standalone 'sustainability' report, the idea is that one report should capture the strategic and operational actions of management in its holistic approach to business and stakeholder 'wellbeing'.

There is an increasing recognition that the long-term pursuit of shareholder value is linked to the preservation and enhancement of six different types of capital. These can be broadly related to the three aspects of the TBL:

Aspect of TBL	Type of capital affected
Environmental	**Natural capital** – For example, waste, recycling and emissions.
Social	**Human capital** – Health, skills, motivation of employees. **Social capital** – Relationships, partnerships and co-operation. **Intellectual capital** – Patents, brand value and tacit knowledge.
Economic	**Manufactured capital** – Buildings, equipment and infrastructure. **Financial capital** – Funds available to enable the business to operate. Reflects the value generated from the other types of capital.

The role of the management accountant in IR

The management accountant must produce information that:

- is a balance of quantitative and qualitative information. The IS must be able to capture both financial and non-financial measures
- considers how resources should be allocated
- links past, present and future information. The forward looking nature will require more forecasted information
- considers the impact of relevant laws and regulations and any necessary action
- provides an analysis of opportunities and risks that could impact the future
- Consider how resources should be allocated
- is tailored to the specific situation but remains concise

Environmental management accounting (EMA)

Introduction

Before reporting on environmental matters, e.g. using IR, the organisation needs to identify its existing environmental costs and the effectiveness of its environmental-related activities.

EMA was developed in recognition that traditional management accounting systems were unable to identify or deal adequately with environmental costs resulting in negative environmental and economic impacts.

Definitions

EMA is concerned with the accounting information needs of managers in relation to the organisation's activities that affect the environment as well as environment-related impacts of the organisation. It involves the identification and estimation of the financial and non-financial costs of environmental-related activities with a view to control and reduce these costs.

Categories of environmental cost

Type of environmental cost	Problem
Conventional costs, e.g. energy costs.	Not prioritised since often hidden in overheads.
Contingent costs, e.g. decommissioning costs.	Often ignored due to short-term focus.
Relationship costs, e.g. cost of producing environmental information for reporting.	Ignored by managers who may be unaware of their existence.
Reputational cost, i.e. the cost of failing to address environmental issues.	Ignored by managers who are unaware of the risk of incurring them.

Benefits of EMA

- The focus of EMA is not entirely on financial costs but it also considers the non-financial environmental cost or benefit of any decisions made.
- A clearer understanding of costs should mean that budgets are more realistic and therefore more useful for planning purposes, such as pricing decisions.
- EMA includes environment-related KPIs and targets as part of routine performance monitoring. These will be both financial and non-financial, have an internal and external focus and will relate to both short-term and long-term performance.
- EMA will also often benchmark activities against environmental best practice.

EMA techniques

ABC	• Removes environment-driven costs from overheads and traces them to products or services. • Should result in the identification of cost drivers and better control of costs. • Product costs more realistic resulting in better pricing and decision making.
Lifecycle costing	• Considers the costs and revenues of a product over its whole life rather than one accounting period. • Organisations will have to be financially and environmentally responsible if they have plans to cover these costs. • In order to reduce lifecycle costs may use techniques such as TQM.
Input-output analysis	• Focuses on waste in processes. • Records material inflows and balances this with outflows since 'what comes in, must go out'. • By accounting for outputs in terms of physical quantities and in monetary terms, organisations are forced to focus on environmental costs.

Flow cost accounting

- Aims to reduce the quantity of material, thus reducing costs and having a positive environmental impact.
- Uses not only material flows, but also the organisational structure; looking at material flows and material losses incurred at various stages of the production process.
- Material costs can be divided into different types and the values and cost of each type calculated.

EMA and quality-related costs

In the context of quality, we could consider **environment-related costs as being the costs of ensuring the quality of an organisation's processes or activities in relation to the environment.**

Environment- related cost	Description
Environmental prevention cost	Costs of implementing a quality improvement programme to prevent the negative impact of an organisation's processes or activities in relation to the environment.
Environmental appraisal cost	Costs of quality inspection and testing.
Environmental internal failure cost	Costs arising from a failure to meet quality standards before the product or service reaches the customer.
Environmental external failure cost	Costs arising from a failure to meet quality standards after the product or service reaches the customer.

Exam focus

Exam sitting	Area examined	Question number
Mar/Jun 2023	EMA	2(a)
	Lifecycle costing	2(b)
Sept/Dec 2021	Stakeholders	2(a)
	ESG factors	2(a)
	EMA	2(b)
Sept/Dec 2020	Stakeholders	3(b)
Sept/Dec 2019	Stakeholders	3(a)

chapter

5

Budgeting and control

In this chapter

- Purposes of budgeting.
- Participation in budget setting.
- Budgeting methods.
- Variances.
- Non-budgetary methods for organisational control.
- Forecasting.

Exam focus

Budgeting will assist with performance management since it is an important tool for **planning** and **control** within an organisation and contributes to performance management by providing benchmarks against which to compare actual results (through **variance analysis**) and develop corrective measures.

It is important that the organisation understands the relative merits of the different budgeting approaches and chooses the approach that is most suitable for them.

In addition, it is important to acknowledge that the business environment has become more complex, dynamic, turbulent and uncertain. Organisations need to be more adaptive to change, rather than be stifled by a need to comply with a fixed plan (budget). As a result, there has been an increased use of non-traditional profit-based performance measures in controlling organisations (e.g. beyond budgeting).

Purposes of budgeting

Definition

A **budget** is a quantitative plan prepared for a specific time period.

Budgeting serves a number of purposes:

- Planning
- Responsibility
- Integration
- Motivation
- Evaluation/control

Participation in budget setting

A **top-down** budget is one that is imposed on the budget holder by senior management.

Advantages:

- Avoids budgetary slack
- Avoids dysfunctional behaviour
- Can be quicker
- Senior managers retain control
- Senior managers understand the needs of the whole organisation

A **bottom-up** budget involves divisional managers participating in the setting of the budgets.

Advantages:

- More realistic budgets
- Improved motivation
- Increases divisional manager's understanding
- Frees up senior management resources

Budgeting methods

Definition

Fixed budget – when a budget is prepared for a single level of activity.

Definition

Flexible budget – prepared for a number of levels of activity and can be 'flexed' to the actual level of activity for control purposes.

Definition

Incremental budget – starts with previous period's budget or actual results and adds or subtracts an incremental amount to cover inflation and other expected changes. Can be viewed as a traditional approach.

Suitability	Advantages
• Stable business. • Good cost control. • Limited discretionary costs.	• Quick, easy and low cost. • Motivates managers since targets not changing regularly. • Useful if historical figures accurate and the suitability criteria are fulfilled.

Definition

Zero-based budgeting – requires each cost element to be specifically justified, as though the activities to which the budget relates were being undertaken for the first time.

ZBB stages:

1 Managers identify activities that can be individually evaluated.

2 Activities are described in a decision package.

3 Decision package evaluated and ranked using cost benefit analysis.

4 Results used to allocate resources to various packages.

Suitability	Advantages
• Fast moving business • Historic figures inaccurate • High discretionary costs • Public sector organisations	• Inefficient or obsolete operations can be identified and discontinued. • Resources should be allocated economically and efficiently. • ZBB leads to increased staff involvement at all levels, improving motivation and knowledge. • It responds to a change in the business environment, so useful for a dynamic or fast moving organisation and appropriate if the other suitability criteria exist.

Definition

A **rolling budget** is one that is kept continuously up to date by adding another accounting period (for example, a month or quarter) when the earliest accounting period has expired.

Suitability	Advantages
• Fast moving organisation • New business • Any organisation that needs cost control	• Budgeting and control should be more accurate. • Better information to base the manager's appraisal on. • Fixed period budget will always exist. • It forces management to take the budgeting process seriously.

Activity-based budgeting (ABB)

Before we look at ABB, let's begin by recapping our costing knowledge from PM.

Absorption costing (AC)

Aims to calculate the full production cost per unit.

Assumes production overheads are driven by the level of activity.

Activity based costing (ABC)

Aim also to calculate the full production cost per unit.

Recognises the diversity and complexity of modern production meaning that not all production overheads are driven by level of activity.

Steps in ABC

1 Group production overheads into activities **(cost pools)**, according to how they are driven.

2 Identify **cost drivers** for each activity.

3 Calculate an overhead absorption rate **(OAR)** for each activity.

4 **Absorb** activity costs into products.

5 Calculate the **full production cost/unit** and profit/(loss).

Advantages of ABC	Disadvantages of ABC
• Provides a more accurate cost per unit leading to better pricing, cost control and decision making. • Better insight into what drives costs resulting in better control of costs. • Can be applied to all overhead costs and to service costing.	• Cost may exceed benefit. • Limited benefit if overhead minimal or mainly driven by level of production. • Allocating overheads to specific activities and determining cost drivers is difficult. • Assigning responsibility for cost pools is difficult. • Limited benefit if activity costs already well controlled or process is efficient. • Customers may not tolerate changes such as price increases or changes to product specifications.

Definition

Activity based management (ABM) is the use of ABC information for management purposes to improve **operational** and **strategic** decisions. **ABM** applies ABC principles in order to satisfy customer needs using the least amount of resources.

Operational ABM

Helps operational managers make decisions that can **improve operational efficiency** and hence performance:

- Can reduce or eliminate activities that don't add value.
- Find ways to continually improve the value-adding activities.
- May identify design improvements.

Strategic ABM

Uses ABC information to decide which products to develop and sell based on profitability.

- Can assist with customer profitability analysis (CPA).
- May assist in improving relationships with customers and suppliers.

BE CAREFUL:

- Some operational activities and strategic decisions will have an implicit value that is not necessarily reflected in the financial value.
- The cost may outweigh the benefit.

Definition

Activity based budgeting (ABB) uses the costs determined in ABC to prepare budgets for each activity.

The cost driver for each activity is identified. A forecast is made of the number of units of the cost driver that will occur in the budget period. Given the estimate of the number of units of the cost driver, the activity cost is estimated.

ABB advantages	ABB disadvantages
• Draws attention to cost of overhead activities, which can be a large proportion of total operating cost. • Recognises that by controlling cost drivers, costs can be better managed and understood. • Can be used to identify CSFs. • Can provide useful information for a TQM environment (links cost and quality).	• Time and effort required. • Staffing issues such as cost of training required and potential resistance to change. • Cost of adapting IS to collect correct information. • Not suited to organisations not using ABC. • Difficult to identify responsibility for activities and hence accountability for achieving budget set. • It could be argued that many overhead costs are not controllable in the short-term.

Variances

Variances are a key element of management control.

1 Targets and standards are set.

2 Actual performance is measured.

3 Actual results compared to flexed standard, using variance analysis.

4 'Significant' variances investigated and appropriate action taken.

Exam focus

In APM, you may be asked to calculate a variance, although it is likely that calculation marks will account for only the minority of marks available for a question on variances. Do spend a little bit of time reviewing the variances covered in PM to ensure you are comfortable with the calculations and the meaning of each variance. Without being able to do this first, it will be difficult to address the requirements of the APM syllabus area on variances.

Planning and operational variances

The variances calculated can be divided into planning and operational elements if the original budget was inappropriate.

- The **planning variance** is the difference between the original and the revised budget (due to inaccuracies in the original budget, not controllable by operational manager so should not be held accountable for these).
- The **operational variance** is the difference between the revised standard and the actual performance (due to decisions of operational managers and therefore they are controllable by them and can be held accountable to these variances).

Non-budgetary methods for organisational control

The use of traditional budgeting (including methods such as incremental budgeting) is comfortable and predictable and it may still have its place in organisations.

However, there are also many **weaknesses and limitations of traditional approaches to budgeting:**

- Costly and time consuming.
- Focus is on short-term results.
- Insufficient external focus.
- Top-down approach to strategy and decision-making (hierarchy of control and accountability).
- Less suited to modern organisations where change is the new norm and the importance of an empowered and adaptive organisation is paramount.

One example of a non-budgetary approach is **beyond budgeting**.

Beyond budgeting (BB) is the generic term given to the body of practices intended to replace traditional budgeting as a management model.			
Principles:			
Governance and transparency For example, bound to a common cause by the mission and set of values rather than controlled by a central plan.	**Accountable teams** For example, teams empowered to make decisions and any budgets used are bottom-up.	**Goals, targets and rewards** For example, using a range of relevant financial and non-financial, external and internal, targets linked to shareholder wealth.	**Planning and control** For example, planning is continuous (using rolling budgets) and the focus is on the future.

Beyond budgeting advantages	Beyond budgeting disadvantages
• Planning continuous and organisation more proactive. • Lower costs due to move away from concept of budget entitlement. • Targets more challenging and with an external focus. • Managers not constrained by traditional budgets and fixed resources. • Creates IS which provide fast and open information.	• Planning, co-ordination, performance evaluation and rewards systems become more complicated. • Effort and motivation low if targets and benchmarks viewed as unachievable. • Goals may be less clear or not communicated. • Staff resistance. • May be difficult to adopt culture of decentralisation. • Costly investment in IS may be needed.

Forecasting

The hi-low method	Analyses, for example, a semi-variable cost into its fixed and variable elements. These elements are then used to forecast the total cost at any level of activity.
Regression analysis	Used to estimate the line of best fit and can be used for forecasting whenever a linear relationship is assumed between two variables.
Time series analysis	Makes assumptions about past patterns in data, such as the general trend, seasonality and cyclical variations, to forecast figures.
The learning curve model	Takes account of the learning curve effect to forecast the average labour time/unit or labour cost/unit.

Exam focus

Exam sitting	Area examined	Question number
Sept 2022	Comparison of ZBB and incremental budgeting	1(i)
	Interaction of ZBB and kaizen	1(iii)
Mar/Jun 2019	Budgeting methods	3(a)
	ABB and ABM	2 and 3(a)
	Variances	3(b)

chapter

6

Business structure and performance management

In this chapter

- Organisational forms.
- Complex business structures.
- The needs of services.
- Business integration.
- Business process re-engineering (BPR).

Exam focus

In this chapter we will look at the information and information system requirements of **different business structures**. We will also discuss the implications of a particular structure for performance management.

An important element of structure is **business integration**. Performance management can improve as a result of linkages between people, operations, strategy and technology. This chapter reviews two important frameworks for understanding business integration; Porter's value chain and McKinsey's 7s model.

The chapter also introduces the topic of **business process re-engineering**. This is the fundamental redesign of business processes and, amongst other things, it can result in a change of structure.

Organisational forms

	Functional organisations (centralised)	Divisional organisations (decentralised)
Information needs (the IS should aid these needs)	• Data passed from functional to upper levels. • Data aggregated at the highest level before feedback given.	• Information needs to be available lower down organisation due to the high level of autonomy. • Top management need information to measure and control divisions.
Advantages for performance management	• Better standardisation and control. The IS should aid this communication. • Defined career path and sense of belonging for specialists. • Lower costs since roles are not duplicated.	• Easier to grow/diversify. • Clear responsibility for decisions. • Training of general managers. • Speed and quality of decision making. • Top management can focus on strategy.
Problems for performance management	• Empire building and conflicts between functions. • Slow decision making. • Hard to grow/ diversify.	• Loss of control and co-ordination (goal congruence not achieved). • Determining accountability difficult. • Difficult to appraise divisions due to inter-dependence. • Difficult to re-apportion head office costs. • Cost of duplicated functions.

Responsibility accounting

Definition

Responsibility accounting is a system of accounting based on the identification of individual parts of a business (responsibility centres) which are the responsibility of a single manager. The areas of responsibility may be a cost centre, profit centre or investment centre.

- Each division will be a responsibility centre.
- Divisional managers should only be held accountable for those areas of responsibility they can control.
- The information systems should ensure that costs and revenues can be traced to those responsible.

Network (virtual) organisation	
Information needs	• The organisation needs to establish shared goals and contractual agreements. • Those responsible for regulating performance will need information for decision making. • Each party needs feedback on its performance. The IS will need to be sophisticated with the ability to gather and process the information from all parties.
Advantages for performance management	• Flexibility to meet project needs. • Can exploit market opportunities. • Can compete with larger organisations. • Lower infrastructure costs.
Disadvantages for performance management	• Difficult to agree common goals and measures. • Planning and control difficult. • Monitoring of the workforce difficult. • Information gathering difficult if IS not compatible. • Loss of competitive advantage if partners work for competitors. Many of the problems can be addressed using a service level agreement (SLA).

Complex business structures

Definition

A **joint venture (JV)** is a separate business entity whose shares are owned by two or more business entities.

Why form a JV?

- To facilitate development of new products or expansion into new markets.
- Sharing of resources, costs, risks, skills, experience and intellectual property.
- Flexibility since business retains its unique identity and partners are only bound for the pre-agreed period.

Planning difficulties

- Difficult to agree on common goals, measures and targets.
- Difficult to agree how to share, e.g. resources, accountability etc.
- Planning difficult, e.g. due to different locations or IS.
- Difficult to form an effective JV board.

Performance measurement difficulties

- Difficult if no integrated or common IS.
- Measurement and reporting of performance, difficult if partners are unwilling to share information.
- Different opinions on how measures should be calculated or determined.

Control difficulties

- Hard to compare actual performance (performance measurement may be difficult) to target performance (establishing this will be difficult).
- Attributing accountability for performance (good or bad) is difficult.

Strategic alliances

Definition

A **strategic alliance** is similar to a JV but a **separate business entity is not formed**.

Comparison to a JV

The **reasons for forming a strategic alliance** and the **challenges for performance management and measurement** are very **similar to those discussed for a JV**.

A **relative benefit** of a strategic alliance over a JV is greater flexibility since the strategic alliance is not constrained by the reporting and compliance requirements of a separate legal entity.

Additional problems more specific to a strategic alliance are:

- Independence is retained.
- Security of information may be more of a concern.
- Does not have other benefits of a separate legal entity.

Complex supply chains

Definition

A **supply chain** consists of a network of organisations. Together they provide and process the necessary raw materials firstly into work-in-progress and then into finished goods for distribution and sale to the customer. As organisations have grown in size and complexity, **complexity** in the supply chain is becoming **more commonplace**.

Benefits for performance management	Challenges for performance management
• Harnessing of the knowledge and skills of partners. • Builds positive relationships based on the joint quest to, e.g. improve quality. • Partners work together to fulfil customer needs in an optimum way, driving competitive advantage. • Reduces reliance on one or a small number of partners.	• Difficult if the supply chain is more 'complicated' than 'complex'. • Each partner will have their own goals and these will have to be aligned to a common purpose. • Skills required to manage the relationships. • Measuring performance may be difficult, e.g. what to measure, collection of information.

The needs of services

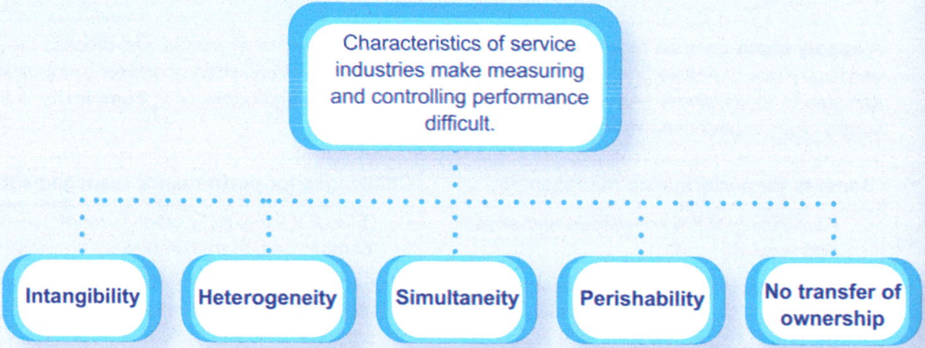

These differences will result in different objectives and CSFs. Appropriate performance measures should be established.

Business integration

Definition

- Business integration is an important part of business structure. It means that all aspects of the business must be aligned to secure the most efficient use of the organisation's resources so that it can achieve its objectives effectively.
- Rather than focusing on individual parts of the business, the whole process should be considered (two possible frameworks are explored below).

Porter's value chain

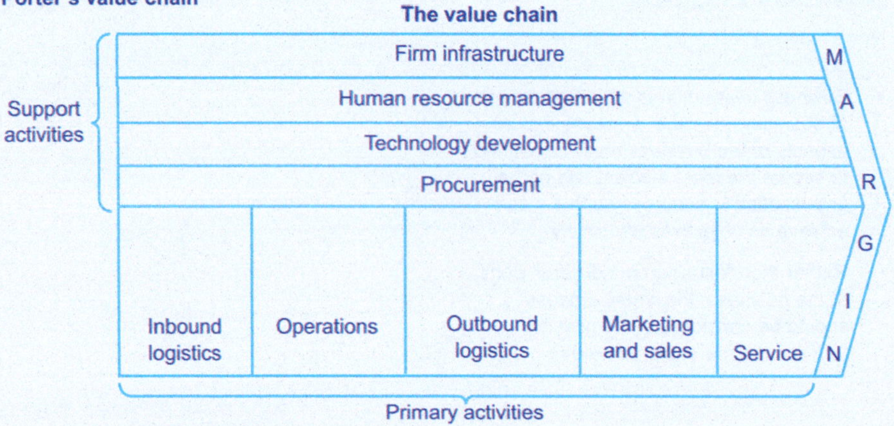

Uses in performance management:

- Used to identify **strengths and weaknesses** as part of strategic analysis.
- Used to identify **CSFs** within each activity and establish appropriate **measures**.
- Shows linkages between activities leading to **common information systems**.
- Considers **support activities** which may have been dismissed as overheads.
- Extend to include the value chain of customers and suppliers (**value system**).

Mckinsey's 7s model

- Describes an organisation as consisting of seven interrelated internal elements which must be aligned to secure success.
- Used to identify elements to realign to improve performance or to maintain alignment and performance during a period of change.
- Three hard elements (systems, strategy and structure) and four soft elements (skills, staff, style and shared values).

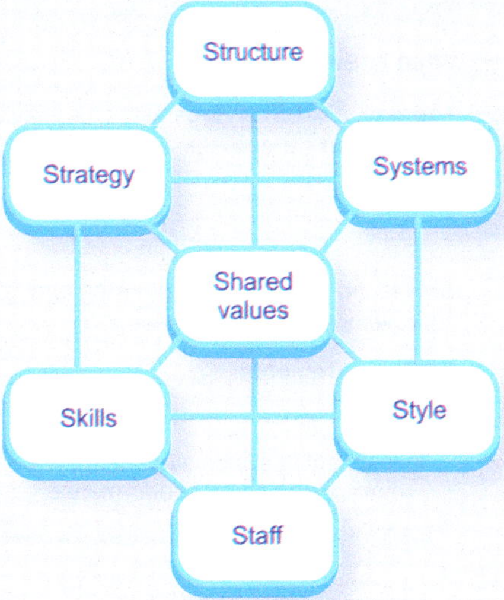

Business process re-engineering (BPR)

What is BPR?

The way in which an organisation's activities (as per the value chain) and interrelate constitute an organisation's processes.

Definition

BPR is the fundamental rethinking and radical redesign of business processes to achieve dramatic improvements in performance.

BPR requirements:

- Investment in systems to adequately monitor and control performance
- Employee training
- Clear communication and leadership
- Rewards aligned to new roles and performance measures
- A change in culture to a process view with process teams
- Greater automation and use of IT

Advantages for performance management	Disadvantages for performance management
• Encourages long-term strategic view. • Revolves around customer's needs. • Allows workers more autonomy. • Can help eliminate unnecessary activities and make a process cheaper.	• Additional costs, for example of new information systems or training. • Staff cuts/cost cutting demoralising. • Staff feel devalued if role changes. • Lost co-ordination if middle managers stripped out. • Often utilises outsourcing which has its own problems. • Processes may be merely automated and not redesigned. • Backward looking.

Exam focus

Exam sitting	Area examined	Question number
Sept/Dec 2023	BPR	2(a)(b)
Dec 2022	BPR	2(b)
Mar/Jun 2022	Service level agreements	3(a)
Sept/Dec 2021	BPR	3(a)
Sept/Dec 2020	Organisational forms and complex structures	3(a)
	7S model	2(a)
Sept/Dec 2019	Value chain	1(iv)

chapter

7

Information systems and developments in technology

In this chapter

- Management information.
- Developing management accounting information systems.
- IT developments.
- Big data.

Exam focus

Managers need access to good information in order to be able to effectively plan, direct and control the activities that they are responsible for. The first part of this chapter focuses on management information and on the development and importance of an effective management accounting information system.

The chapter then goes on to look at some IT developments and discusses how advancements in technology have enabled organisations to better measure and control performance and to improve performance.

The final part of the chapter discusses the development of big data and data analytics and its impact on the role of the management accountant. It discusses the methods of data analysis and data analytics and some of the ethical issues involved.

Management information

Managers need access to 'good' information for planning, control and decision making. Good information should be 'ACCURATE':

- **A**ccurate
- **C**omplete
- **C**ost < benefit
- **U**nderstandable
- **R**elevant
- **A**daptable (or **A**ccessible)
- **T**imely
- **E**asy to use

Sources of information are internal and external. Internal information is from a known origin, should meet the organisation's needs and should be easier and cheaper to collect but external information should also be used alongside it.

Types of information include financial or non-financial, quantitative or qualitative.

Developing management accounting information systems

Definition

A management information system (**MIS**) converts internal and external data into useful information which is then communicated to managers at all levels and across all functions to enable them to make timely and effective decisions for planning, directing and controlling activities.

There are a number of types of MIS:

Executive information system (EIS)

- Gives senior managers access to internal and external information
- Presented in a user-friendly summarised form
- Option to drill down to a greater level of detail

Decision support system (DSS)

- Aids managers in making decisions
- Predicts the consequences of a number of possible scenarios
- Manager then uses their judgement to make the final decision

Transaction processing system (TPS)

- Records, summarises and reports daily transactions to aid operational managers' decisions.

Expert system

- Hold specialist knowledge
- Allow non-experts to interrogate for information, advice and recommended decisions

Quality MIS

A MIS should produce quality information, consistent with the characteristics of 'good' information.

Definition

A lean approach aims to identify and eliminate waste in the MIS and improve the efficiency and flow of information to users. A **lean MIS** aims to get the right thing to the right place at the right time.

The **5 Ss concept** is often associated with lean principles and aims to create a workplace (or in this case, a MIS) which is in order:

S	Example of application to MIS
Structure (sometimes called sort)	Structured and ordered IS allowing quick access by those who require it and to fulfil their needs.
Systemise (sometimes called simplify)	The IS should improve efficiency and accuracy with items arranged for ease of use and duplication eliminated.
Sanitise (sometimes called scan)	Removal of obsolete or duplicated data. Also, only producing reports for people who need them or are authorised to receive them.
Standardise	Establishing an optimum standard for producing output reports and then applying this consistently.
Self-discipline (sometimes called sustain)	Motivating employees to continually perform the above will result in continuous improvement of the IS.

The importance of IS integration

It is important that IS (and the information produced by them) do not exist in isolation but rather the IS in the organisation should be connected and integrated.

Definition

A **data silo** is when data exists in separate areas of the organisation or in separate IS and does not connect up with or integrate with other organisational data or information systems.

Issues of data silos	How to address the issues
• May result in **duplicated information** – this is inefficient and therefore costly and the information may not be 'good'. • The **data may be held in one silo only**, creating a barrier to collaboration and co-ordination since: – information is inaccessible or invisible to other systems or users – different parts of the business start to work independently, perhaps prioritising their own objectives – if users identify a need to access other information and to co-ordinate with other users, this process will be slow, time consuming and costly.	Data silos occur naturally as organisations grow can be overcome through: • the **adoption of new technology**, e.g. cloud or network technology. • by **changing the organisation's culture** and processes to encourage the sharing of information.

The need for continual systems development

Information and accounting systems need to be developed continually to maintain or improve performance.

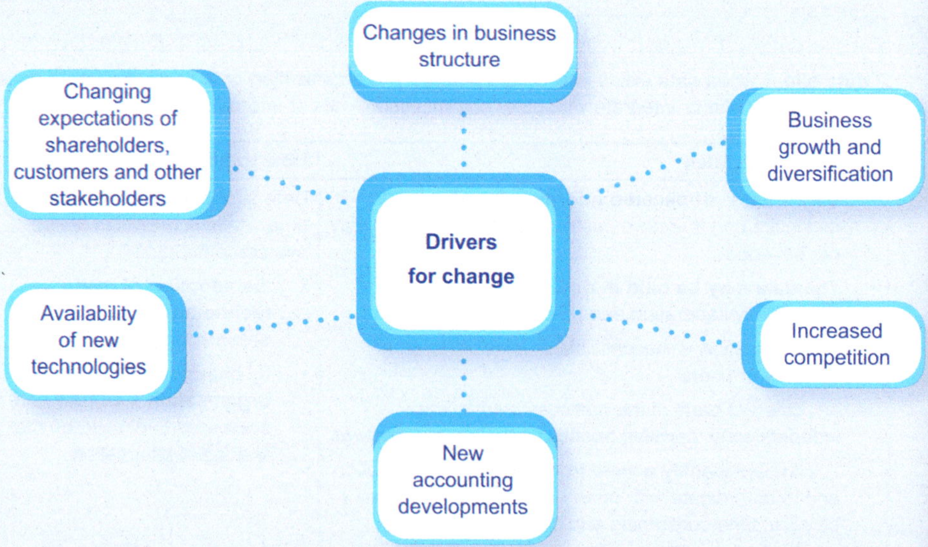

IT developments

Exam focus

There has been a wealth of IT developments in recent times. You are not expected to be IT experts, rather to consider how the developments may enhance performance but also to understand the risks and challenges they present.

Networks

Facilitate the transfer of information across the organisation.

- Intranets, extranets and the internet all rely on netwok technology.
- All of the IT developments discussed in this chapter reply on networks.

Cloud technology

Definition

Storing and accessing data and programs over the internet instead of on a computer's hard drive.

Benefits	Risks
• Flexibility • Scalability • Lower costs • Improved security • Flexible working • Lower environmental impact	• Organisational change • Contract management • Security threat • Reliance

Data warehouses

Definition

Data is combined from multiple and varied sources into one comprehensive, secure and easily manipulated store. Data can be accessed to suit the user's needs and can be mined to understand patterns and correlations.

Advantages	Disadvantages
• Reduced duplication and storage • Improved integrity • Flexible to user's needs • Aligned across the organisation and can be linked to suppliers' and customers' systems • Instant access to data	• Cost of system and training • Failure/ security breach more catastrophic

Enterprise resource planning system (ERPS)

Definition

An ERPS is an example of a **unified corporate database**. It integrates data from all different parts of the organisation into a single system that allows all users to access the same information, to see an overall picture of performance and helps inform business decisions.

Benefits (Includes the advantages of databases but more specifically the below)	Impact on role of management accountant
• Senior managers have access to data all in one place. • Decision support features aid management decisions. • Improved flow/communication of information across the organisation. • Plans use of resources across the organisation. • Less duplication of data. • Can extend to include customer and supplier software.	• Less routine assembly of information. • More analysing the information to gain insight. • Management accountants will work more alongside others in the organisation.

Knowledge management systems (KMS)

Definition

A KMS is any type of IT that helps to capture, store, retrieve and use knowledge to enhance the knowledge management process.

Examples include:

- groupware
- intranets/extranets
- data warehouses
- decision support systems (DSS).

Management accountants will play an important role in knowledge management.

Customer relationship management (CRM) systems

Definition

Technology needed to gather the information needed to attract and retain customers.

Most systems are based on a database of customer information. The data is analysed so that any gaps in customer related performance can be identified and appropriate strategies and targets can then be set.

Radio frequency identification (RFID)

Definition

Radio receivers are used to tag items and hence keep track of assets.

Benefits include access to better real time information, improved accuracy and control.

Process automation

Definition

The technology enabled transformation of business processes previously carried out by human workers, aimed at implementing consistency, quality and speed whilst delivering cost savings.

- Automation of low value, low skilled, repetitive tasks will free up time for higher value adding activities.
- Technology developments are now enabling automation of more complex processes.

Internet of things

Definition

The network of 'smart' devices with in built software and connectivity to the internet allowing them to constantly monitor and exchange data.

Artificial intelligence (AI)

Definition

AI is an area of computer science that emphasises the creation of intelligent machines that work and react like human beings.

Definition

Machine learning is a subset of AI. Computer code mimics how the human brain works, using data and experiences to improve their function over time in making predictions and recommendations.

Definition

An **algorithm** is a sequence of instructions to perform a computation or solve a problem. The term algorithm includes simpler sets of rules as well as more advanced AI or machine learning code.

Big data

Definition

Big data refers to extremely large collections of data that may be analysed to reveal patterns, trends and associations.

Characteristics include **variety**, **volume**, **velocity**, **veracity** and **value (The 5Vs)**.

Benefits of effective data management	Risks associated with big data
• Fresh insight and understanding • Performance improvement • Market segmentation and customisation • Improved decision making • Innovation • Improved risk management	• Skills required not available • Data security • Time spent measuring relationships that have no value • Poor veracity leading to incorrect conclusions • Cost of analytics hardware and software • Technical difficulties integrating big data system and current system • Keeping abreast of system developments

Big data analytics

Data analytics is used to extract the value from big data.

Definition

Data analytics is the process of collecting, organising and analysing large sets of data to discover patterns and other information that an organisation can use for future decisions.

The volume of data as well as its importance is increasing and therefore it is important to make sense of this data.

Definition

Data visualisation allows large volumes of complex data to be displayed in a visually appealing and accessible way that facilitates the understanding and use of the underlying data.

Data analysis methods

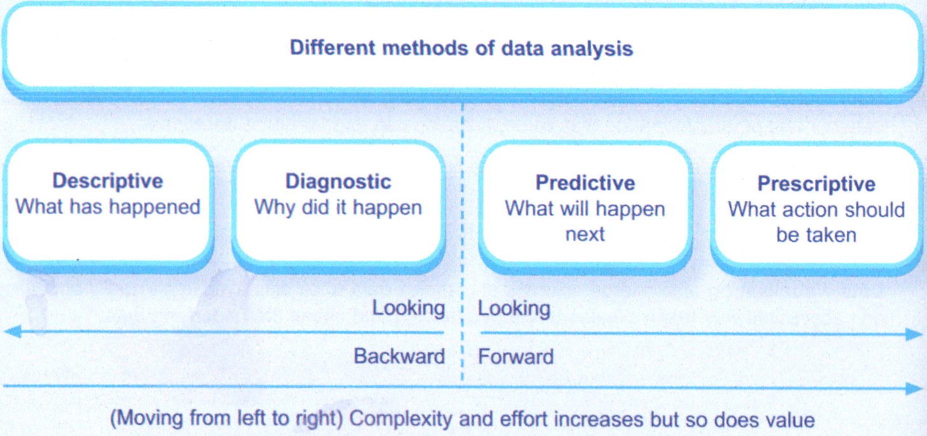

Tools for data analysis

A number of tools can be used for each of the respective methods of data analysis. For example, **descriptive analysis** may use **simple statistical tools** (e.g. percentages) and **visual tools** (e.g. graphs) where as **prescriptive analysis** may use **AI and machine learning algorithms**.

The following tools can be used for **data analysis**:

Definition

Linear regression is a statistical technique that attempts to identify factors that are associated with the change in the value of a key variable.

Definition

Regression analysis is a technique for estimating the line of best fit given a series of data.

Definition

Time series forecasting can establish not only underlying trends but also seasonal variations. These can be used to make predictions about the future.

Definition

Expected value uses the probabilities of outcomes to choose the course of action with the most beneficial expected value.

Definition

Standard deviation measures how clustered or dispersed a data set is in relation to the mean.

Definition

A decision tree is a diagrammatic representation of a multi-decision problem, where all possible courses of action are represented, and every possible course of action is shown.

Definition

Sensitivity analysis considers the effect of changing one variable at a time. **Simulation** improves on this by looking at the impact of many variables changing at the same time.

Alternative methods of data analytics

The data analysis methods above will use data in a variety of structured and unstructured forms:

Text analytics →	Existing text is analysed to gain invaluable insights.
Image analytics →	The extraction of useful information from (mainly digital) images.
Video analytics →	Analysis of historical/real-time video content to gain valuable insights.
Voice analytics →	Used to automatically identify and analyse speech including words and phrases.

Definition

Sentiment analysis (also known as opinion mining) determines the emotional tone behind a series of written (text) or verbal (voice) words to understand attitudes, opinions and emotions.

Ethical issues associated with information collection and processing

The amount of personal data available to and used by organisations means that the privacy, sensitivity and security of this data are very significant considerations in modern business.

General Data Protection Regulation (GDPR) was introduced to address the growing significance of ethical information collection and processing. The legislation details a number of principles about data (for example, it should be used fairly, lawfully and transparently).

A **voluntary** commitment to corporate digital responsibility may also be used.

Definition

Corporate digital responsibility (CDR) is the application of CSR to the digital world and involves a commitment to protecting both customers and employees and ensuring that new technologies and data are used both productively and wisely.

The ethics of big data, AI and algorithms – Algorithms produce an outcome or answer that organisations and people may rely on for making a decision. However, most algorithms do not explain how they arrived at that answer. These are known as 'black box' algorithms.

Definition

One way to gain public trust is to use **explainable AI**. This generates an audit trail alongside the answer, showing the working of the algorithm and other supporting information, to explain how the answer or conclusion is arrived at. The information is available in a human-readable way, rather than being hidden in code.

The role of the management accountant in big data

Management accountants are well placed to provide organisations with the competencies needed to realise the value in the data.

1. **Data manager** – establishing metrics, working with data scientists to ensure the information is collected and used, reporting back to senior managers.

2. **Data scientist** – help meet the challenges of advanced data analytics. The management accountant will more often partner with data scientists.

3. **Data champion** – the management accountant can help cascade this influence from board level throughout the organisation.

4. **Finance business partner** – partner with business managers, IT professionals and data experts from across the organisation to support performance improvement through harnessing the value of big data.

Exam focus

Exam sitting	Area examined	Question number
Mar/Jun 2023	Data ethics	3(c)
Sept 2022	Costs and benefits of RFID	1(iv)
Mar/Jun 2022	Management accounting information, 'good' information	1(iii)
Sept/Dec 2020	IT developments	2(b)
March 2020	IT developments	1(iii)

chapter

8

Performance reports for management

In this chapter

- Reports for performance management.
- Presentation techniques.
- Problems dealing with quantitative data.
- Problems dealing with qualitative data.

Exam focus

An important component of this good information will be the performance reports produced for management. The output reports produced from a management information system might include overall performance reports for managers or they may be more specific and tailored to the manager in question. Importantly, the performance reports need to be tailored to suit the needs of the users of those reports. The qualities of a good performance report are discussed in the first part of this chapter.

The chapter then moves on to discuss data visualisation. This was touched upon in Chapter 7 and is also relevant here since it can be used to present the information in the performance report in a user friendly and accessible way.

The final part of the chapter focuses on the types of information, firstly looking at the common mistakes and misconceptions that people make when using numerical data for performance measurement and then secondly the chapter discusses qualitative information. Qualitative information is highly subjective and hard to pin down and is therefore often ignored to the detriment of the quality of the performance report. However, although it is difficult to record and process data of a qualitative nature these factors still need to be considered when making a decision.

Reports for performance management

Considerations when designing a performance report:

- The **purpose** of the report should be considered – does it reflect the mission and objectives?
- The **layout** should be user friendly and avoid information overload.
- The **information** must match the purpose. A range of financial and non-financial (quantitative and qualitative), internal and external information should be included.
- The **audience** should be considered – the report should be relevant and understandable for the audience.

Note: Do not be constrained by this list. Ensure your points are relevant to the given scenario.

Presentation techniques

Definition

Data visualisation allows large volumes of complex data to be displayed in a visually appealing and accessible way that facilitates the understanding and use of the underlying data.

For example, a dashboard displaying live KPIs.

An effective data visualisation tool should consider **purpose, audience, information** and **layout.**

Benefits:

- Accessible
- Real time
- Performance optimisation
- Insight and understanding

Problems dealing with quantitative data

There are a number of common mistakes and misconceptions that people make when using numerical data for performance management:

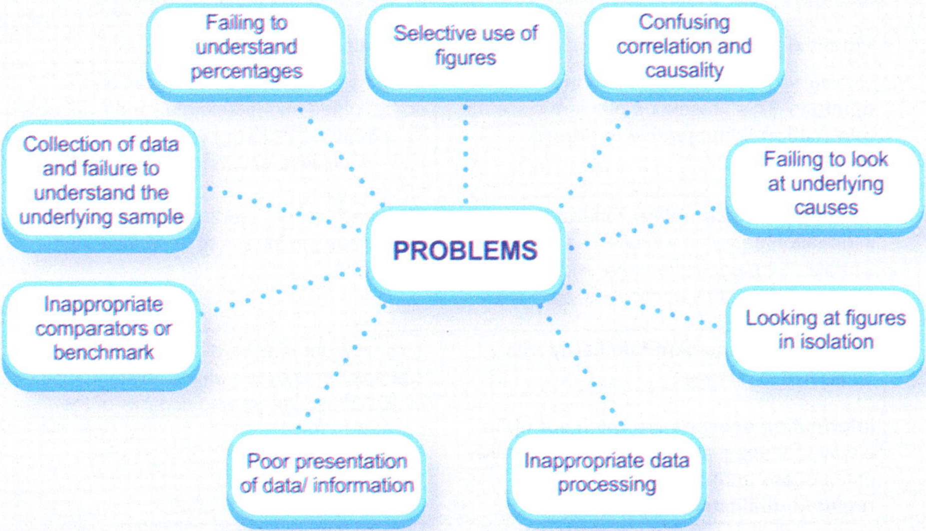

Problems dealing with qualitative data

Definition

Qualitative data is information that cannot normally be expressed in numerical terms.

Potential problem	Potential solution
Qualitative information is **often in the form of opinions**. This presents a problem since the **information is subjective in nature**.	Such opinions must be collected and co-ordinated into meaningful 'good' information, for example by looking at trends, transformation into quantitative data or using data analytics.
Data may be incomplete. Qualitative information gathered will often be from a sample of the population only and may not be representative of all employees' opinions.	The organisation needs to find a way to encourage the individual to provide their opinion.
A **lack of management familiarity** with qualitative information. **Information systems are often set up in a way** that adequately captures quantitative data but **are unable to generate the required qualitative information.**	This problem may be overcome using, for example, employee training, systems upgrades or additional checks and controls of the qualitative data.

Exam focus

Exam sitting	Area examined	Question number
Mar/Jun 2023	Performance reports	1(i)
Dec 2022	Performance reports	1(i)
	Qualitative data	1(ii)
Sept/Dec 2021	Performance reports	1(i)(ii)
	Quantitative and qualitative data	1(i)(ii)
Mar/June 2021	Performance reports	1(a)
March 2020	Performance reports	1(i)
Sept/Dec 2019	Performance reports	1(i)
	Quantitative and qualitative data	2(a)

chapter

9

Human resources aspects of performance management

In this chapter

- Introduction to human resource management (HRM).
- Management styles.
- The purpose of reward systems.
- Methods of reward.
- Linking reward schemes to performance measurement.

Exam focus

This chapter looks at the link between human resource management and performance measurement and considers the impact of the employee reward system on the behaviour of employees and on the performance of the organisation as a whole.

It also discusses the accountability issues that might arise from performance measurement systems.

It concludes by looking at how management style needs to be considered when designing an effective performance measurement system.

Introduction to human resource management (HRM)

Definition

HRM is the strategic and coherent approach to the management of an organisation's most valued assets: the people working there who individually and collectively contribute to the achievement of its objectives for sustainable competitive advantage.

HRM includes the recruitment, selection and induction of employees, the development of policies relating to human resources (e.g. reward systems), the management and development of employees (e.g. through training and development and through performance measurement and the appraisal system) and the termination of employees. In APM, the **focus is on performance measurement and reward practices**.

Today, employees are seen **less as an expensive necessity** and more as a **strategic resource** that may provide the organisation with **competitive advantage** and assist it in **achieving its mission and objectives**.

Management styles

Hopwood identified three distinct management styles of performance appraisal. The style needs to be considered when designing an effective performance measurement system.

Management style	Advantages	Disadvantages
Budget constrained – manager's reward linked to achievement of short-term financial targets, for example ROCE used as a target.	• Should ensure short-term targets are met. • It may also motivate managers, who find it easier to focus on short-term targets.	• Short-termism. • Stress and difficult working relationships. • Lack of flexibility. • Stifles ingenuity. • Can result in manipulation of data.
Profit-conscious – manager's reward linked to achievement of long-term profitability, for example project NPV used as a target.	• Compared to budget constrained should result in a focus on long-term profitability, greater flexibility, less stress and better working relationships and less manipulation of data. • May motivate and help retain employees if rewards linked to achievement of long-term targets.	• Loss of short-term control could result in, for example, cash flow issues. • May ignore non-financial aspects such as ESG issues.

Non-accounting – Manager's reward linked primarily to achievement of the non-financial aspects that drive long-term performance. For example, employee satisfaction and productivity.	• Focus is on causes (such as customer satisfaction) rather than effects (profitability) which should lead to long-term success. • Compared to budget constrained should result in greater flexibility, less stress and better working relationships and less manipulation of data. • Meaningful targets may motivate and help attract/retain employees.	• Short and long-term financial implications of behaviour may be neglected.

Note: The potential for the **'manipulation'** of data is discussed above and in a number of subsequent chapters. In the exam, exercise caution when including this as part of your answer. Accounting data is not simple to manipulate; there are checks and balances and audit requirements in place. 'Manipulation', if it does exist, would more likely be in the form of the accounting method used or policy changes than fraud.

The purpose of reward systems

Definition

Reward schemes are the monetary, non-monetary and psychological payments an organisation provides for its employees in exchange for the work they perform.

A **key purpose** of reward systems is **to assist in the achievement of strategic objectives**. The reward system offered to employees should ideally include a method that is aligned with and motivates the employee to achieve the organisation's plan, objectives and mission since:

- **what gets measured, gets done**
- **what gets measured and fed back, gets done well and**
- **what gets rewarded, gets repeated.**

Note: One performance measurement system that makes the link between the achievement of corporate strategy and the management of human resources is the **Building Block model** (Chapter 13).

Other purposes include:

- To ensure the recruitment and retention of appropriately skilled and experienced staff.
- To provide a fair and consistent basis for rewarding employees.
- To motivate staff and maximise performance.
- To reward performance through promotion or progression.
- To control salary costs.
- To comply with legal requirements and ethical obligations.
- To ensure the employee's attitude to risk is aligned with that of the organisation.

Risks of poorly designed reward schemes

Strategic risk	If the reward scheme is not aligned to the organisation's goals, the result may be a failure to attract and retain the employees needed for organisational success.
Behavioural risk	If the reward scheme is not aligned to the required employee behaviours, the result may be rewarding inappropriate or unproductive behaviour.
Financial risk	Inadequate reward cost management.
Legal and ethical risk	Non-compliance with legal/regulatory requirements or societal/ethical expectations can result in employee claims, regulatory action and/or reputational damage.

Methods of reward

Method	Advantages	Disadvantages
Basic pay – the minimum amount the employee receives (e.g. per hour or year).	• Easy and cheap to administer. • Helps meet employee's basic needs. • Competitive rate helps attract and retain the best employees.	• No alignment to mission and strategic goals. • Does not motivate employees to improve performance.
Benefits – a wide range of rewards other than wages or pensions, such as company cars or health insurance.	• Can be tailored to the employee. • May be a cheaper method. • Tool to attract and retain the best employees. • Can compensate for lower amounts of other rewards.	• No alignment to mission and strategic goals. • Employees may not want the benefits offered. • May be costly to provide and/or difficult to administer.

Method	Advantages	Disadvantages
Executive share option schemes – gives (normally senior) employees the right to purchase shares at a specified exercise price after a specified time-period in the future.	• Should align management and shareholder interests. • A tool to attract and retain the best employees. • May encourage risk-averse directors to take positive action. • Can compensate for lower amounts of other rewards. • Can be a tax-efficient method.	• Can encourage risk-seeking behaviour. • It may give directors an incentive to manipulate share price. • Costly and time consuming to administer.
Performance-related pay – based on the level of performance achieved. Types include pay that is linked to individual performance, group performance or to profit and also the use of commission.	• Motivates employees to achieve strategy, if aligned to this. • Motivates employees to improve performance. • A tool to attract and retain the best employees. • Can compensate for lower amounts of other rewards.	• Can be subjective and inconsistent. • Can be viewed as unfair if based on team/company performance. • Can be stressful for employee if they rely on this pay for basic needs. • Can be complicated, costly and time consuming to administer.

Linking reward schemes to performance measurement

Part of the employee's reward (e.g. a bonus or pay increase) may be performance-related and linked to the achievement of pre-agreed objectives.

Appropriate **SMART** targets (performance measures) should be set for employees. The targets should be:

- Specific – i.e. not vague.
- Measurable – the achievement should be measurable.
- Attainable – i.e. not too difficult or impossible to achieve.
- Relevant – to the organisation's mission and objectives.
- Time-bound – i.e. should be achieved by a specified date.

In **addition to being SMART**, targets should be:

- controllable by the employee.
- a prioritised, small set.
- rewarded appropriately.

Benefits and problems of linking reward schemes to performance measurement

Benefits	Problems
• Makes it clear to all employees that employee performance creates organisational success. • This will benefit both the employee (motivated by the reward to work towards this success) and the employer (reward is given only if the organisation achieves its goals). • Targets that are SMART, controllable, small in number, prioritised and rewarded will be considered fair and consistent. • Effective schemes also attract and retain the employees valuable to an organisation. • Creates an organisation focused on continuous improvement ('what gets rewarded, gets repeated').	• Targets that are not SMART, are uncontrollable, large in number or not prioritised or rewarded, will be considered unfair and will not motivate employees. • Employees may become highly stressed if a significant proportion of their income is performance related. • Employees may prioritise the achievement of the reward, which can impact their risk appetite. • If the targets are not aligned to the organisation's overall objectives, employees will have an extra incentive towards dysfunctional behaviour. • It may be difficult to decide if targets should be based on individual, team, division or group performance.

Problems of poorly designed performance measurement systems

A poorly designed performance measurement systems can result in wrong signals and dysfunctional behaviour:

Misrepresentation	**Gaming**	**Sub-optimisation**	**Misinterpretation**
Myopia	**Measure fixation**	**Tunnel vision**	**Ossification**

Exam focus

Exam sitting	Area examined	Question number
Sept/Dec 2023	Management approaches	3(A)
	Reward schemes	2(C)
Dec 2022	Executive share option schemes	3(b)
Sept 2022	Reward scheme linked to EVA	2(b)
Sept/Dec 2021	Reward schemes	1(iv)
	Reward schemes	3(b)

chapter

10

Financial performance measures in the private sector

In this chapter

- Objective of a profit-seeking organisation.
- Financial performance measures.
- Short- and long-term financial performance.

Exam focus

In the exam, you may be required to look at performance measures in a variety of contexts. In this chapter, we focus on the principal measures used by the private sector. The emphasis will be on financial measures (non–financial measures will be reviewed in Chapter 13).

Objective of a profit-seeking organisation

Shareholders are the legal owners of the company.

Main objective of a business is to **maximise shareholder wealth**.

Financial performance measures

Introduction

- Financial performance measures are used to measure the performance of the whole organisation, its divisions (Chapter 11) and key projects.
- Financial performance can be assessed in terms of profitability, liquidity and risk.

Exam focus

- APM is all about a **critical approach**. It is about selecting from the range of indicators that you know from PM and using those that are most appropriate to the scenario.
- Indicators are **meaningless if calculated in isolation** but should be compared to, for example, a previous period or an appropriate benchmark (such as a competitor or to an industry average) or to any targets set.
- In addition to calculating the numbers, the examining team will expect you to give **performance management advice based on what you have calculated**.

Measuring profitability (whole organisation)

Profitability measure	Advantages	Disadvantages
Gross and operating profit (Can calculate as a margin)	• Information readily available. • Easy to compare between companies. • Widely understood. • Ignores uncontrollable figures.	• Poor correlation to shareholder wealth. • Can be distorted by accounting policies. • Operating profit less useful for highlighting product profitability issues.
ROCE (return on capital employed) = operating profit ÷ (capital employed) × 100	• Easy to calculate. • Figures readily available. • Measures how well a firm is utilising resources invested in it. • Often used by external investors/analysts.	• Poor correlation to shareholder wealth. • Differences between companies or accounting policies make comparisons less meaningful. • Possible dysfunctional behaviour.
EPS (earnings per share) = (PAT – preference dividends) ÷ weighted average number of ordinary shares	• Easy to calculate and widely understood. • Calculation precisely defined by accounting standards.	• Poor correlation to shareholder wealth. • Accounting treatment may distort measure.

EBITDA, i.e. earnings before interest, tax, depreciation and amortisation (and write-offs such as goodwill)	• A measure of underlying performance since it is a proxy for cash flow generated from operating profit. • Ignores tax and interest since these are externally generated and therefore not relevant to the underlying success of the business. • Ignores depreciation/ amortisation (a write off over several years. • Easily calculated and understood.	• Poor correlation to shareholder wealth. • Comparison between organisations difficult due to differences in accounting policies and the calculation of an absolute figure. • It can be easily manipulated. • Ignores changes to working capital or amount of non-current asset replacement needed.

Other profitability measures (whole organisation)

Can be used alongside main measures such as ROCE and include the following:

EVA, ROI and RI	Chapter 11
Asset turnover	$\frac{\text{Sales}}{\text{Capital employed}}$
Dividend cover	$\frac{\text{PAT}}{\text{Dividends paid during the year}}$
Dividend yield	$\frac{\text{Dividend per share}}{\text{Current share price}} \times 100\%$
P/E ratio	$\frac{\text{Share price}}{\text{EPS}}$
Earnings yield	$\frac{\text{EPS}}{\text{Share price}} \times 100\%$
Return on equity	$\frac{\text{Net profit after tax}}{\text{Average shareholder's equity}} \times 100\%$

Liquidity ratios

There is often a trade-off between liquidity and profitability. Liquidity needs to be considered alongside profitability to ensure the organisation can meet its short-term obligations.

Current ratio	$\frac{\text{Current assets}}{\text{Current liabilities}}$
Acid test (quick ratio)	$\frac{\text{Current assets} - \text{inventories}}{\text{Current liabilities}}$
Inventory period	$\frac{\text{Average value of Inventory}}{\text{Cost of sales}} \times 365$
Receivables period	$\frac{\text{Average receivables}}{\text{Sales revenue}} \times 365$
Payables period	$\frac{\text{Average payables}}{\text{Purchases}} \times 365$

Risk ratios

These ratios measure the ability of the company to meet its liabilities

Financial gearing A higher figure = higher financial risk – If profits fall the organisation is less able to finance its LTD (and pay preference dividends)	$\frac{\text{LTD + Preference share capital}}{\text{Shareholders' funds}} \times 100\%$ or $\frac{\text{LTD + Preference share capital}}{\text{LTD + Preference share capital + Shareholders' funds}} \times 100\%$
Operating gearing A higher figure = higher business risk – A fluctuation in sales volume might lead to falling profits as fixed costs are not covered.	$\frac{\text{Contribution}}{\text{PBIT}}$
Interest cover A low interest cover indicates the company may have difficulty financing its debts if profits fall.	$\frac{\text{PBIT}}{\text{Interest charges}}$

Note: LTD = Long-term debt

Short- and long-term financial performance

Short-term financial performance measures are used for:	BUT a focus on short-term financial performance can damage shareholder wealth, for example:	Therefore, need steps to reduce short-termism, for example:
• control purposes, for example variance analysis • determining rewards • assessing the quality of past decisions and the impact of decisions yet to be made.	• investment in new assets is cut • investment in training and development is cut.	• use a range of financial and non-financial measures • switch from a budget-constrained style • give managers share options or link bonuses to long-term performance • use long-term measures such as NPV and IRR • use VBM • reduced decentralisation.

Measuring long-term profitability (key projects)

Profitability measure	Advantages	Disadvantages
NPV • Based on DCF analysis. • Looks at present value of cash inflows less present value of outflows of project. • Any project with a positive NPV is viable.	• Aligned to shareholder wealth. • Considers time value of money. • Can allow for risk. • Cash flows less subject to manipulation than profits. • Considers whole life of project.	• Difficult to calculate/ understand. • Absolute figure makes comparison difficult. • Based on a number of assumptions. • Challenging to use for target-setting (profit based measures still often used).
IRR • Discount rate when NPV = 0. • Accept project if IRR > firm's cost of capital.	• Provides alternative to NPV when cost of capital of project is uncertain. • Percentage aids comparison.	• Possible to get multiple rates of return. • More difficult to calculate and to understand than NPV.
MIRR • Represents the actual return generated by a project.	• Eliminates the problems associated with IRR. • As for IRR.	• More difficult to calculate and to understand than NPV.

Exam focus

Exam sitting	Area examined	Question number
Sept 2022	EBITDA	2(a)
Sept 2022	NPV and MIRR	3(b)
Sept/Dec 2021	Assessing financial performance	1(iii)

chapter

11

Divisional performance appraisal and transfer pricing

In this chapter

- Problems associated with divisional structures.
- Structuring divisions as responsibility centres.
- ROI.
- RI.
- EVA.
- Value-based management.
- Transfer pricing.

Exam focus

Business structure (including divisional structures) was covered in Chapter 6. A feature of modern business management is the practice of splitting a business into semi-autonomous units with devolved authority and responsibility. Such units could be described as divisions, subsidiaries or strategic business units (SBUs) but the principles are the same.

This chapter will review some of the methods available for appraising divisional performance. Before looking at these methods, the problems associated with divisional structures, the concept of responsibility accounting and the types of responsibility centre, will be reviewed.

The chapter then covers the value-based management approach to performance management and how this might help to address some of the issues of short-termism already discussed.

The chapter concludes with a discussion of transfer pricing, focusing on why a transfer price may be needed and considerations when setting a transfer price.

Problems associated with divisional structures

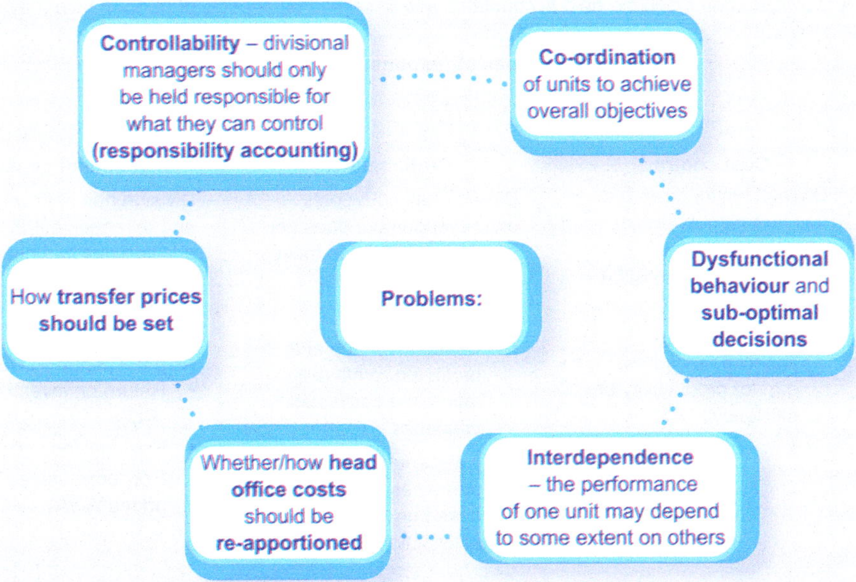

Structuring divisions as responsibility centres

A manager should only be held accountable and assessed on aspects of performance they control.

Types of responsibility centre

Cost centre

Division incurs costs but has no revenue stream.

Measures:

- Costs, e.g. cost ratios and variances
- Relevant non-financial measures, e.g. for productivity or efficiency.

Profit centre

Division has both costs and revenues but does not have the authority to make investment decisions.

Measures:

- Costs, revenues and profit, e.g. profitability ratios and cost/sales variances
- Relevant non-financial measures, e.g. based on customer satisfaction.

Investment centre

Division has both costs and revenues but in addition has authority to make investment decisions.

Measures:

As profit centre PLUS

- Return on investment (ROI)
- Residual income (RI)
- Economic value added (EVA).

ROI

- Divisional equivalent of ROCE.

$$ROI = (\text{controllable operating profit} \div \text{controllable capital employed}) \times 100$$

- **Decision rule:** If ROI > target cost of capital then accept divisional project or appraise division as performing favourably.
- The **advantages and disadvantages** are as for ROCE. Two of the disadvantages, i.e. dysfunctional behaviour and a tendency to hold onto old assets are key drivers for one of the alternative measures (RI or EVA) being used.

RI

Residual income (RI)	Advantages	Disadvantages
Controllable operating profit X **less: imputed interest** X **RI** X • Imputed interest = controllable capital employed x cost of capital. • **Decision**: accept the project, if the RI is positive.	• Reduces the problems of ROI, i.e. dysfunctional behaviour and holding on to old assets. • Easy decision rule. • Highlights cost of financing a division. • Different cost of capitals can be applied to different divisions based on their risk profiles.	• It does not always result in decisions that are in the best interests of the company (EVA is a superior measure). • Absolute figure does not facilitate comparison. • Different accounting policies can confuse comparisons. • It is difficult to decide upon an appropriate cost of capital. • May encourage manipulation of profit and capital employed.

EVA

Economic value added (EVA)	Advantages	Disadvantages
NOPAT X **Adjusted value of capital employed at start of year × WACC** (X) **EVA** X • A similar but superior measure to RI. • **Decision:** accept the project if the EVA is positive.	• EVA is consistant with NPV and should create real wealth for shareholders. • The adjustments made avoid distortion by accounting policies and should therefore result in goal congruent decisions. • Emphasises cost of financing to division's manager. • Long-term value-adding expenditure can be capitalised, removing any incentive for managers to take a short-term view. • Easy decision rule.	• Requires numerous adjustments to profit and capital employed figures. • Its complexity may be poorly understood by managers who as a result are less likely to achieve EVA targets. • Some of the adjustments (e.g. economic depreciation) may be difficult to measure. • Many assumptions made when calculating WACC. • Absolute measure (as is RI) so divisional comparisons difficult. • Based on historical data where as shareholders are interested in future performance.

How to calculate EVA

NOPAT

Controllable operating profit	X
Add:	
accounting depreciation	X
increase in provisions	X
non-cash expenses	X
advertising, r&d, employee training	X
Deduct:	
economic depreciation	(X)
decrease in provisions	(X)
amortisation of advertising, r&d and employee training	(X)
tax paid including lost tax relief on interest	(X)
NOPAT	X

Adjusted value of capital employed at the beginning of the year

	$
Capital employed at beginning of year	X
Adjust to reflect replacement cost of assets	X/(X)
Adjust to reflect economic and not accounting depreciation	X/(X)
Add back value of provisions in the year	X
Add back non-cash expenses in the previous year	X
Add NBV of advertising, R&D and employee training at end of previous year	X
Adjusted value of capital employed at beginning of year	X

WACC

WACC = (proportion of equity x cost of equity) + (proportion of debt x post tax cost of debt).

Value-based management (VBM)

Definition

VBM is an approach to management whereby the company's strategy, objectives, culture and processes are aligned to help the company focus on **key drivers of shareholder wealth** and hence maximise this value.

- VBM takes the **interests of its shareholders as its primary focus**.
- It begins with the view that the **value of a company** (and hence shareholder wealth) is the **total value of its discounted cash flows.**
- To measure performance under VBM a **single overall organisational metric** is established, **such as EVA, market value added (MVA)** or **shareholder value added (SVA).**
- Then **value drivers are identified.** These are activities linked to long-term shareholder value that:
  - managers can influence and control
  - cascade throughout all levels of the organisation and across all divisions
  - link to staff/manager objectives
  - cover financial and non-financial areas of performance.

Implementing VBM

1. **Strategy developed** to maximise shareholder value, measured using a single overall organisational metric. Value drivers defined.
2. **Performance targets created** for value drivers.
3. **Operational plans** – targets are assigned to specific employees and specific operational plans are defined.
4. **Performance measures and rewards** (aligned to these targets) are created for all levels of staff.

VBM evaluation

Advantages	Disadvantages
• Focus on value (not profit) and therefore takes the interests of shareholders as its primary focus. • Is long-term and forward-looking. • Value drivers are established and aligned at all levels of the organisation and across all divisions. • Controllable targets created and assigned to specific employees. • Specific plans are created to help the employee achieve these targets. • Performance metrics (financial and non-financial) are created that are compatible with these targets and that motivate employees.	• Requires a cultural shift (and perhaps training). • Shareholders may need to be educated to understand VBM. • Requires a change adept organisational culture plus commitment and leadership from the board. • It may be difficult to identify value drivers. • May need to adapt MIS to take account of new measures. • Can become an exercise in valuing everything and changing nothing.

Note: Since EVA and NPV are two of the key measures used in VBM, the advantages and disadvantages of these will also be relevant here.

Transfer pricing

Definition

The transfer price is the price at which goods and services are transferred from one division to another in the same organisation.

Characteristics of a good transfer price:

- Goal congruence
- Fair for divisions
- Autonomy for divisions
- Assists bookkeeping
- Minimises global tax liability
- Considers spare capacity

General rules for setting transfer prices

Perfect competition in market for intermediate product

- Transfer at market price.
- Include any small adjustments, e.g. savings on delivery.

Surplus capacity

- Minimum price selling division will accept = marginal cost.
- Maximum price the buying division will pay is the lower of the external purchase price (if available) and the net marginal revenue.

Production constraints

- Minimum price selling division will accept = marginal cost + lost contribution from other product.
- Maximum price the buying division will pay is the lower of the external purchase price (if available) and the net marginal revenue.

Note:

- The selling division will want to cover some/all of the **fixed costs** and recognise a **% profit** whereas the buying division will want to pay the minimum amount acceptable to the selling division.
- When using the cost, the **standard cost** should be used rather than the actual cost to aid planning and prevent inefficiencies being passed on to the buying division.

Issue (fairness)

- Selling division wants to use total cost to ensure recover fixed overheads and would prefer to recognise a % profit.
- Buying division will not want to be charged for fixed costs or a % profit.

Solutions

- **Two part tariff** – Transfer price is marginal cost/unit (favoured by buying division) + periodic lump sum to cover fixed costs (thus keeps the selling division happy).
- **Dual pricing** – The buying and selling division recognise two different transfer prices. This will be perceived as fair by both divisions but the problem with this is that a period end adjustment to the accounts will be needed.

International issues

Taxation	If the buying and selling division are based in different countries, the organisation may try to increase profits by adjusting the transfer price to take advantage of different tax rates in each country. Tax authorities rule that the organisation **treat the transactions as having taken place at a fair arm's length price** and revise profits accordingly.
Remittance controls	A country's government may impose **restrictions on the transfer of profits** from domestic subsidiaries to foreign multinationals.
Protectionist measures	A country's government may introduce measures to protect local manufacturers from competition from imported goods. Include **import tariffs** or a requirement that all **transfers to be at arm's length price**.
Exchange rates	Fluctuations in exchange rates between the buying and selling country will **alter the price** and may affect the division's decision to buy or sell. It will also make **planning and budgeting more difficult. Divisional managers may require an adjustment to the transfer price** to reflect this uncontrollable movement but this results in difficulties calculating, recording and understanding the price.

Exam focus

Exam sitting	Area examined	Question number
Sept/Dec 2023	ROI/RI calculation and evaluation	3(c)
Dec 2022	Transfer pricing	1(iii)
Sept 2022	EVA	2(a)
	Reward scheme linked to EVA	2(b)
Sept 2022	VBM	3(a)
Mar/Jun 2022	ROI/RI calculation and evaluation	1(i)
Mar/Jun 2022	Transfer pricing	2
Mar/Jun 2022	VBM	3(b)
Mar 2020	Divisional performance including ROI, RI and EVA	2(b)
	VBM	2(a)
Sept/Dec 2019	Divisional performance including ROI, RI and EVA	1(ii)

chapter

12

Performance management in not-for-profit organisations

In this chapter

- What is a not-for-profit organisation?
- Problems associated with performance management.
- Measuring public sector performance using value for money (VFM).
- The use of benchmarking (league tables) and targets in the public sector.

Exam focus

You need to be able to discuss the issues which affect not-for-profit organisations and the implications of these for performance management.

What is a not-for-profit organisation?

Not-for-profit (NFP)
organisations exist in:

Private sector

For example, charities, sports clubs.

Public sector

For example, healthcare, defence.

- Their **objective is not the maximisation of shareholder wealth.**
- Instead, it is to **maximise the benefit to beneficiaries**.

Problems associated with performance management

Problem	Possible solution
Non-quantifiable costs and benefits (in monetary terms)	• Cost benefit analysis (CBA), i.e. try to quantify in monetary terms all of the costs and benefits associated with a decision. • Assess **value for money (VFM)**.
Assessing the use of funds Many NFP organisations (particularly public sector organisations) do not generate revenue; rather funds are invested in them (by government for public sector organisations). Need to assess if these funds are being put to the best use but this can be difficult.	An assessment of the use of funds can be carried out using a **VFM** framework.

Problem	Possible solution
Potential conflict due to multiple and diverse objectives NFP organisations do not have an objective of maximisation of shareholder wealth. Instead, they are seeking to satisfy the needs of a range of stakeholders. Multiple stakeholders give rise to multiple and diverse objectives and these objectives may conflict.	• **Prioritise** the objectives of the organisation. • Make **compromises** so that the needs of all stakeholders are taken into account to a greater or lesser degree. • Achievement of the established set of objectives can be measured using a **VFM** framework.
Impact of politics Public scrutiny of some sectors, such as health and education, make them a prime target for political interference.	• Difficult – need to encourage politicians to have a long-term focus. • League tables and targets are commonly used in the public sector as a method of managing and measuring performance.

Measuring public sector performance using value for money (VFM)

NFPIs in NFP organisations

A key component in assessing VFM is the use of non-financial performance indicators (NFPIs).

Financial performance measurement remains important to NFP organisations. However, NFPIs are particularly important for measuring performance in NFP organisations due to the following reasons:

- NFP organisations do not have the underlying financial objective to maximise profit in order to maximise shareholder wealth, making financial indicators of performance less relevant.
- Many NFP organisations do not have a revenue stream and it can be difficult to define a cost unit or to quantify the benefits. This makes traditional financial indicators less relevant or easy to use.
- Many NFP organisations have numerous stakeholders with multiple and often diverse objectives. Many of these objectives are non-financial in nature and therefore NFPIs are required to measure performance.
- Financial objectives are less relevant in NFP organisations. NFPIs are more relevant for measuring the achievement of the objectives of NFP organisations and capturing aspects of the organisation's mission that are fundamentally non-financial and subjective.

Assessing value for money using the 3 Es

Economy	Efficiency	Effectiveness
Are the appropriate quantity and quality of resources (inputs) bought at the lowest cost possible?	How well are the inputs (resources used) converted into outputs? This means optimising the process by which inputs are turned into outputs to maximise the output generated from the units of resource used.	How well do these outputs (actual results) help achieve the stated objectives of the organisation?

- Appropriate (financial and non-financial) **performance indicators** should be chosen for each E.
- **Comparison** should be made internally to historic performance and perhaps benchmarked against suitable external organisations.
- The aim of VFM is to achieve an appropriate balance between the 3 Es but this can often be difficult to achieve and **conflict** may arise.
- Sometimes a **fourth 'E', equity**, is included.

The use of benchmarking (league tables) and targets in the public sector

Benchmarking and league tables

Benchmarking is undertaken by many public sector organisations. The **results from a benchmarking** exercise can be used to **rank organisations in a league table**.

Advantages	Disadvantages
• Stimulates competition and the adoption of best practice. • Monitors and ensures accountability. • Performance is transparent. • Allow consumers to make choices. • Many different areas of performance summarised into one weighted average score.	• Dysfunctional behaviour if targets not aligned to mission. • Only measures relative performance. • Differences between organisations make comparisons and accountability difficult. • What areas/weightings to use in the scoring system to arrive at the ranking? • The quality of information output dependent on quality of data input. • Poor ranking impacts employee morale and public trust and can result in worsening future performance. • Can become measuring rather than learning exercise. • Measures chosen may be based on what is practical and not meaningful. • Costly and time consuming. • May encourage creative reporting

Targets

Benefits	Issues
Targets should improve: • efficiency, effectiveness and economy • accountability and transparency • responsiveness to stakeholders and • employee motivation, if linked to reward.	• Central control • Difficulty level • All or nothing • Too many targets • Targets not always appropriate • Cost • Lack of ownership of targets • Gaming • Conflict

Exam focus

Exam sitting	Area examined	Question number
Sept/Dec 2023	Performance management in NFPOs	1(i)
	Value for money	1(ii)
	Benchmarking (league tables) and targets	1(iii)
Sept/Dec 2020	Performance management in NFPOs	1(ii)
	Benchmarking (league tables) and targets	1(iii)

chapter

13

Non-financial performance indicators

In this chapter

- Introduction to non-financial performance indicators (NFPIs).
- The balanced scorecard.
- Fitzgerald and Moon's Building Block model.
- The performance pyramid.

Exam focus

In Chapters 10 and 11 we looked at a wide range of financial performance measures. In order to fully appraise the performance of an organisation, and to understand if the best techniques are being used to drive its success, it is useful to use a range of financial performance indicators (FPIs) and non-financial performance indicators (NFPIs).

Introduction to non-financial performance indicators (NFPIs)

Limitations of financial performance indicators

- Short-termism
- Internal focus
- Do not convey the whole picture
- Backward looking
- Manipulation of results

Solution – use NFPIs and FPIs

In order to overcome these issues the following should be used to assess performance:

- **FPIs** (these reveal the results of actions already taken) and
- Non-financial performance indicators (**NFPIs**) (reflect the long-term viability and health of the organisation and will drive future financial performance).

NFPIs and business performance

NFPIs play a key role in a number of areas.

Management of human resources (HR)	Product and service quality	Brand awareness and company profile
• Recruitment and selection – time to fill a position. • Training and development – training feedback. • Motivation – employee satisfaction scores. • Reward systems – adherence to laws and regulations.	• The quality of incoming supplies. • The quality of work completed. • Customer satisfaction.	• Customer awareness. • Customer opinions.

The balanced scorecard

Allows managers to look at the business from four important perspectives.

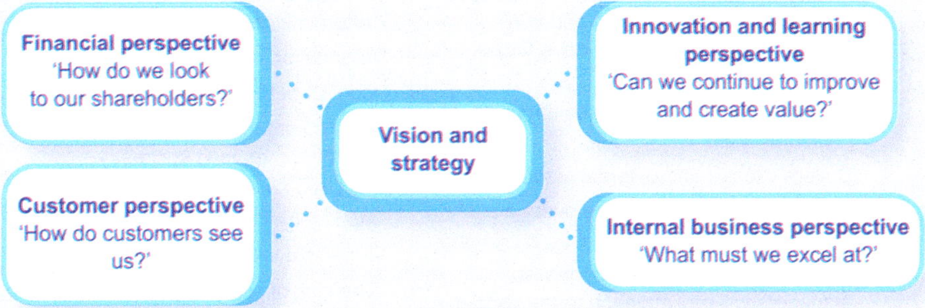

Within each perspective the organisation should **identify a series of goals (CSFs)** and **establish appropriate measures (KPIs)** in line with the overall vision and strategy.

Evaluation of the balanced scorecard as a performance measurement tool

Advantages of balanced scorecard	Disadvantages of balanced scorecard
• Includes financial measures – these reveal the results of actions taken and non-financial measures – these drive future financial performance. • Distorting performance harder if multiple measures used. • Covers internal and external matters. • It is flexible and can change over time to reflect changing priorities. • 'What gets measured gets done' so managers will pay attention to the various aspects of performance that they know they are being appraised on. • Links achievement of long-term and short-term objectives to achievement of strategy and vision.	• Difficult to record and process non-financial (often qualitative) data. • Information overload. • Conflict between measures. • Poor communication to employees and manager threatens success. • Lack of commitment by senior management. • Time/cost involved. • The lack of some key perspectives, for example ESG. • Measures chosen many not align with strategy/vision. • Focuses on strategic level.

Implementing the balanced scorecard

Make the strategy explicit

- Strategy forms the basis of the scorecard.
- May involve strategy mapping.

Choose the measures

- Align measures with strategy.
- Relationships between measures must be clearly understood.

Define and refine

- Put performance measures into place.
- Scorecard becomes the language of the company.

Deal with people

- People and change must be properly managed.
- Rewards aligned to achieve targets.

Fitzgerald and Moon's Building Block model

What is the Building Block model?

A performance measurement system for the service sector based on three building blocks.

DIMENSIONS

6 dimensions (CSFs)

Downstream results:

1 Financial performance
2 Competitiveness

Upstream determinants:

3 Quality of service
4 Flexibility
5 Resource utilisation
6 Innovation

Need suitable metrics (**KPIs**).

STANDARDS

These are the targets set for the metrics (KPIs) chosen. Standards should have three characteristics:

1 **Ownership.**
2 **Achievability.**
3 **Fairness.**

REWARDS

The model makes a link between the achievement of corporate strategy and the management of HR.

To ensure **employees are motivated to meet the standards,** the standards need to be:

1 **Clear** (SMART, prioritised, not too many)
2 Linked to **controllable** factors

and the reward should be desirable.

Advantages of building block model	Disadvantages of building block model
The first five advantages discussed for the balanced scorecard are relevant. In addition: • It differentiates between downstream results and upstream determinants. • Tailored for service industry. • Targets are set in such a way to engage and motivate staff, i.e. due to ownership, achievability and fairness. • Reward system should optimally motivate staff due to it being clear and linked to controllable factors.	The first seven disadvantages discussed for the balanced scorecard are relevant. In addition: • It is less suitable for non-service companies. • Difficult to see how building blocks link to strategic objectives and mission/vision since there is no explicit link to this.

The performance pyramid

What is the performance pyramid?

- Defines the links between objectives and performance measures at different levels in the organisation.
- Designed to ensure that activities of every department, system and business unit support the overall organisational vision.

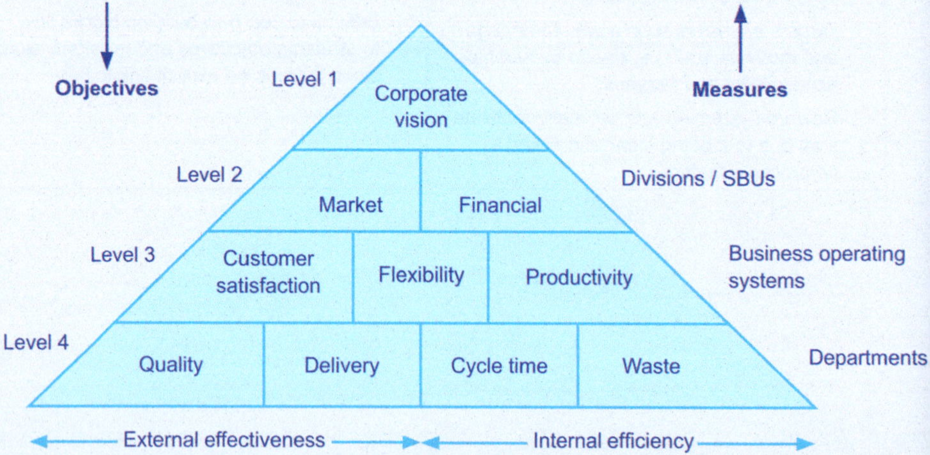

Evaluation of the performance pyramid as a way to link strategy, operations and performance

Advantages of performance pyramid	Disadvantages of performance pyramid
The first five advantages discussed for the balanced scorecard are relevant. In addition: • It is hierarchical requiring senior managers to set objectives and relevant performance measures for each level of the organisation. • It is process focused considering how processes combine to achieve organisational goals. Considers the interaction of measures both horizontally and vertically. • Recognises that financial and non-financial measures can support each other.	The first six disadvantages discussed for the balanced scorecard are relevant. In addition: • The model is quite complicated making the time and resources required significant.

Exam focus

Exam sitting	Area examined	Question number
Mar/Jun 2023	Non-financial performance indicators	3(a)
Dec 2022	Building Block model	3(a)
Sept/Dec 2021	Building Block model	3(b)
Mar/June 2021	Performance pyramid	2
Sept/Dec 2019	Balanced scorecard	2(b)

chapter

14

The role of quality in performance measurement

In this chapter

- What is quality?
- Six sigma.
- Kaizen costing.
- Target costing.
- Total quality management (TQM).
- Just-in-time.
- Lean production.

Exam focus

In today's competitive global business environment, quality is one of the key ways in which a business can differentiate its product or service, improve performance and gain competitive advantage. Quality can form a key part of strategy.

What is quality?

Quality is one of the key ways in which a business can differentiate its product or service, improve performance and gain competitive advantage. It can form a key part of strategy and can be defined in a number of ways.

Definition

Quality can be defined in a number of ways:

- Is the product/service free from errors and does it adhere to design specifications?
- Is the product/service fit for use?
- Does the product/service meet customers' needs?

Definition

A **quality management system** is a set of co-ordinated activities to direct and control an organisation. These quality management activities should be aligned to the organisation's quality objectives and complement the organisation's strategy.

Quality-related costs

Monitoring the costs of quality is key to the operation of any quality improvement programme.

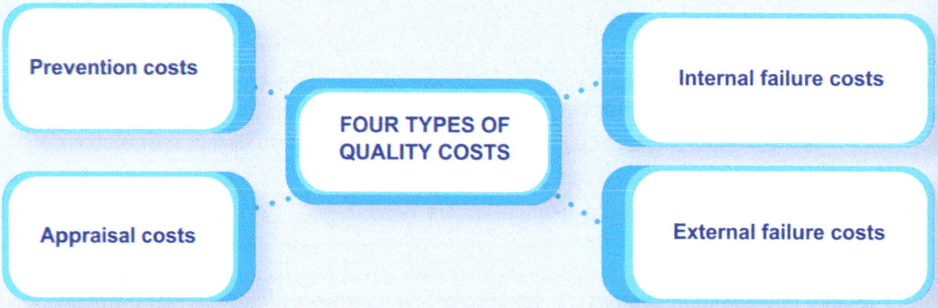

The organisation's costing system should be capable of identifying and collecting these costs.

KPIs should be developed based on the costs of quality and these can be used as a basis for staff rewards.

Six sigma

Aims to reduce the number of faults that go beyond an accepted tolerance level of 3.4 defects per 1 million units produced.

Step 1: **D**efine the process

↓

Step 2: **M**easure existing problems

↓

Step 3: **A**nalyse the process

↓

Step 4: **I**mprove the process

↓

Step 5: **C**ontrol the process

Kaizen costing

Definition

Kaizen costing focuses on producing small, incremental cost reductions throughout the production process through the product's life.

Steps:

1 During the design phase, a target cost is set for each production function.

2 The target costs are totalled to give a baseline target cost for the product's first year of production.

3 As the process improves, cost reductions reduce the baseline cost.

4 Cost reduction targets are set on a regular basis and variance analysis is carried out.

A traditional costing system is inappropriate in a Kaizen environment.

Target costing

Target costing involves setting a target cost by subtracting a desired profit from a competitive market price.

Step 1
A competitive market price is set based on what customers are willing to pay and how much competitors are charging for similar products.

Step 2
The desired profit margin is deducted from this price to arrive at a target cost.

Step 3
The difference between the estimated cost of the product and the target cost is the cost gap.

Step 4
Techniques are used to close the gap. Many of these will be employed at the design stage. The focus should be on features that do not add value (value analysis).

The distinction between Kaizen costing and target costing

Target costing usually occurs at the **beginning** of a product's life. It can achieve large cost reductions at the **design stage** of the product. Kaizen costing is the process of long-term continuous improvement by small, incremental cost reductions **throughout the life** of the product. The **target cost is the starting point for Kaizen costing**, incorporating the idea of only producing what the customer values.

Total quality management (TQM)

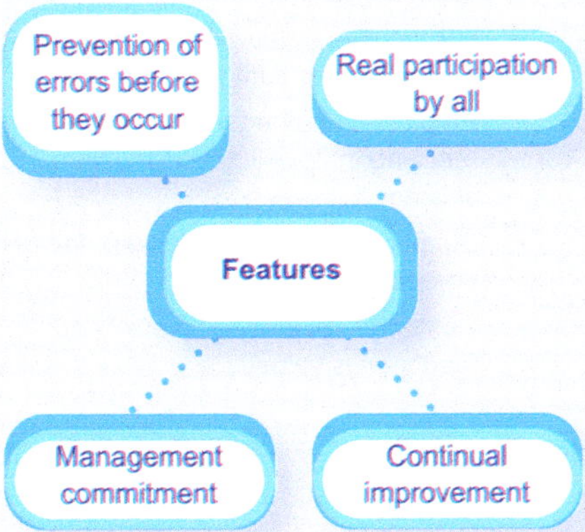

Performance measures should be linked to the programme's CSFs.

Just-in-time

Definition

Just-in-time (JIT) is a system whose objective is to produce or procure products or components as they are required rather than for inventory.

Requirements:

- High quality and reliability.
- Elimination of non-value added activities.
- Speed of throughput to match demand.
- Flexibility.
- Lower costs.

Traditional performance measures such as inventory turnover will be replaced with more appropriate measures, such as total head count and productivity.

Lean production

Definition

Lean production is a philosophy of management based on cutting out waste and unnecessary activities including:

- Over-production
- Inventory
- Waiting
- Defective units
- Motion
- Transportation
- Over-processing

Characteristics of lean production:

- Production in smaller batches leading to quick set up and flexibility.
- HR focuses on empowering staff, giving them a career path and job for life.
- Employees trained in all aspects resulting in flexibility and problem solving.
- Supplier expertise harnessed, fair price agreed and JIT operated.
- Customer flexibility delivered and feedback is valued.

The 5 **Ss** concept is often associated with lean principles and has the aim of creating a workplace which is in order.

5 Ss	**Explanation**
Structure (sometimes called sort)	Introduce order where possible.
Systemise (sometimes called simplify)	Arrange and identify items for ease of use and systematic approach.
Sanitise (sometimes called scan)	Be tidy, avoid clutter.
Standardise	Find the best approach and then be consistent in using it.
Self-discipline (sometimes called sustain)	Do above daily.

Exam focus

Exam sitting	Area examined	Question number
Sept 2022	Kaizen costing	1(ii)
	Interaction of ZBB and kaizen	1(iii)
Mar 2020	Costs of quality	3(b)
	Quality practices	3(a)
Mar/June 2019	Costs of quality	1(c)
	Quality practices	1(b)

Index